CONTENTS

	Inside cover	Portrait: David C. Ward
	2	Editorial
	3	News & Notes
	5	Letter from Silas Gunn

REPORTS

Neil Powell	6	*Rewards of Failure*
Sam Adams	7	*Letter from Wales*
Simon Eckett	9	*Kitaj in the Lake District*
John Greening	9	*Nicholson, Suddenly*
Frank Kuppner	11	*Random Souvenirs of a Fleeting Return to the Continent*

POEMS

Jane Yeh	12	*Seven Poems*
Jean-Paul de Dadelsen	17	*Three Poems* (translated by Marilyn Hacker)
Raymond Queneau	22	*from* Hitting the Streets (translated by Rachel Galvin)
Hester Knibbe	27	*Five Poems* (translated by Jacquelyn Pope)
Anne Stevenson	39	*Two Poems*
Don Coles	40	*Two-Hander*
Janet Kofi-Tsekpo	43	*Six Poems*
Maurice Rutherford	45	*Heinz Gropsmeyer*
Neil Powell	46	*Four Poems*
Pier Paolo Pasolini	51	*Poems Around Town* (translated by N.S. Thompson)
Peter Bland	58	*Wilderness Moments* and *Mr Maui*

ARTICLES

Thomas Day	15	*Variant Editions of Geoffrey Hill's* Mercian Hymns
Roger Caldwell	19	*'The Present King of France is Bald': On Possible Worlds*
Robert Griffiths	25	*Shelley and the Old and New Atheism*
Marius Kociejowski	28	*Once Upon a Time in County Cork*
Adrian May	41	*The Hang of Song: Arctic Monkeys and Clare Pollard*
Carol Rumens	44	*in conversation with Maurice Rutherford*
John Muckle	47	*Out of Town: Robert Duncan, Michael McClure, and The Ground Aslant*
Ian Brinton	54	*Jack Spicer's Words: 'God Must Have a Big Eye'*
Mark Ryan Smith	60	*Two Explorers: Charles Doughty and Hugh MacDiarmid*

REVIEWS

Bernard O'Donoghue	64	*on* The Word Exchange
Judith Chernaik	65	*on Adam Zagajewski*
Will Eaves	66	*on Dan Burt*
Chris Preddle	67	*on Ed Reiss*
Joey Connolly	68	*on Ian Pople*
Gerry McGrath	69	*on* The Ecco Anthology of International Poetry
Alison Brackenbury	69	*on Siân Hughes, Ellen Phethean and Hilary Menos*

| | 71 | Some Contributors |

Cover image: John Ashbery, *Napoleon*, 2009, collage, 12⅜ × 9⅛ inches. Courtesy Tibor de Nagy Gallery, New York

---

Subscriptions (six issues):
£36.00 ($86.00) individuals
£43.00 ($105.00) institutions
to P N Review, Alliance House,
30 Cross Street Manchester M2 7AQ UK

Trade distributors:
CENTRAL BOOKS LTD, 99 Wallis Road, London E9 5LN
email magazines@centralbooks.com

Copyright © 2011 POETRY NATION REVIEW
All rights reserved

ISSN 0144-7076   ISBN 978 1 84777 041 7

General Editor MICHAEL SCHMIDT
Co-ordinating Editor HELEN TOOKEY
News & Notes Editor ELEANOR CRAWFORTH

EDITORIAL ADDRESS:
Michael Schmidt
Department of English
University of Glasgow
5 University Gardens
Glasgow G12 8QH

Manuscripts should be sent to the editorial office and cannot be returned unless accompanied by a self-addressed and stamped envelope or, for writers living abroad, by an international reply coupon.

Typeset in Ehrhardt
by XL Publishing Services
Tiverton, Devon

Printed in England
by SRP Limited, Exeter

EDITORIAL

> By 'exhaustion' I don't mean anything so tired as the subject of physical, moral, or intellectual decadence, only the used-upness of certain forms or exhaustion of certain possibilities – by no means necessarily a cause for despair.
> John Barth

In his 1967 *Atlantic* essay 'The Literature of Exhaustion', a personal *ars poetica* and a celebration of the brittle, essayistic fiction of Borges, the American novelist John Barth declared that the realist tradition was used up. The 'proper novel' has, historically, attempted 'to imitate actions more or less directly, and its conventional devices – cause and effect, linear anecdote, characterization, authorial selection, arrangement, and interpretation – can be and have long since been objected to as obsolete notions, or metaphors for obsolete notions'.

The case for the 'proper novel' is still made, not least by novelists who unapologetically continue working in what they believe to be an unbroken tradition that stretches from Defoe and Fielding to – well, to Howard Jacobson, Hilary Mantel, Nicole Krauss. Barth takes as his first epigraph (post-modern writers can't resist the sound-bites of epigraphs) Borges's, 'The fact is that every writer creates his own precursors. His work modifies our conception of the past, as it will modify the future.' This is a simplified paraphrase of Eliot's high-Modernist argument in 'Tradition and the Individual Talent', which allows to the writer's will considerable latitude, but also imposes on it an expectation: that he or she will be curious and adventurous, and that certain elements within the tradition are non-negotiable, no matter how various the readers' takes on them turn out to be.

In 1967 Cecil Day Lewis, by then a safe pair of hands, was appointed Poet Laureate in succession to John Masefield. Charles Causley was awarded the Queen's Gold Medal. Cholmondeley Awards went to (among others) young Seamus Heaney and 'rising dead' Norman Nicholson, and among the Gregory Award winners were David Harsent and Brian Patten. Highlights of the year included (*plus ça change*) books by Kingsley Amis, Alan Brownjohn, Anthony Thwaite, Brian Patten, Roger McGough... It was Edward Lucie-Smith's finest hour with *The Mersey Sound* making sales history. In such a context the American-inflected work of Thom Gunn in *Touch* and Ted Hughes in *Wodwo* seems to come from quite a different culture, another dimension. Stephen Bann's international *Concrete Poetry* anthology made a very small splash (*frog/pond/plop*). The avant-garde was compelled to seek energies abroad, even though in London, with Fulcrum Press and other small operations, challenging work was published at the margins of a self-satisfied, exhausted centre.

I was an undergraduate in the United States in 1967 and remember, along with the heady subversions of the Students for a Democratic Society, some exciting publishing events, including Robert Lowell's *Near the Ocean* and *Berryman's Sonnets*. Beyond my interests at the time were collaborative works by Ted Berrigan, Ron Padgett and Joe Brainard, Robert Creeley's *Words*, Ed Dorn's *The North Atlantic Turbine*, W.S. Merwin's *The Lice*... Further afield, the man we then knew as *Edward* Brathwaite published *Rights of Passage*, Judith Wright her transitional volume *The Other Half*. Writers who, like David Gascoyne, were attentive to France would have been reading new books by Follain, Jabès, Jaccottet, Ponge, Queneau. In Germany Paul Celan (who had three years left to live) published *Atemwende* and Günter Grass his poems and drawings in *Ausgefragt*.

1967 was followed by the upheavals of 1968. From the anti-Vietnam War activities of an American undergraduate, I transferred to the now forgotten anti-student-file and anti-matriculation demos of a British undergraduate; after the kinds of adolescent anxieties that Philip Roth, remembering Korea, explores in *Indignation* (2008), this was the world of *Lucky Jim* (1954).

How long can a culture survive in a state of exhaustion? Looking at the 2011 prize shortlists, Harsent, Brownjohn and others still contend, immortals, joined by newer immortals. One is reminded of the *New Yorker* advertisement urging readers to 'buy tomorrow's antiques today'. And a kind of perpetual scandal is evident, too: Geoffrey Hill, whose main British honour is elective (the Chair of Poetry at Oxford, in the wake of Ruth Padel's momentary incumbency) is shortlisted and again passed over. Not that it matters to him, but it might matter to poetry readers. A few years ago the judges of a major prize refused to shortlist one of his books because he had dedicated a poem to the late Princess Diana. Certain decorums a contemporary British poet must not transgress, and this was one. Hill called his first Oxford lecture, 'How ill white hairs become a fool and jester'.

There is occasional, accidental justice, however. Posthumously, R.F. Langley was awarded the Forward Prize for Best Single Poem for 'To a Nightingale', which appeared in the *London Review of Books*. Its precision and pace will be familiar to grateful *PN Review* readers. It begins:

> Nothing along the road. But
> petals, maybe. Pink behind
> and white inside. Nothing but
> the coping of a bridge. Mutes
> on the bricks, hard as putty,
> then, in the sun, as metal.
> Burls of Grimmia, hairy,
> hoary, with their seed-capsules
> uncurling. Red mites bowling
> about on the baked lichen
> and what look like casual
> landings, striped flies, Helina,
> Phaonia, could they be?
> This month the lemon, I'll say
> primrose-coloured, moths, which flinch
> along the hedge then turn in
> to hide, are Yellow Shells not
> Shaded Broad-bars. [...]

NEWS & NOTES

Compiled by Eleanor Crawforth

This issue's arresting cover image, the collage *Napoleon, 2009*, features in the new exhibition at the Tibor de Nagy Gallery, New York, of collages by JOHN ASHBERY. This is the poet's second solo exhibition of collages, following his *PNR*-featured début with the gallery in 2008. The new exhibition continues until 3 December 2011 at 724 Fifth Avenue; visit www.tibordenagy.com for details. A full colour spread of Ashbery collages from the exhibition is projected for *PNR* 203.

Ashbery was fascinated in his youth by the collage novels of Max Ernst and the partly collaged Cubist paintings of Picasso and Braque. He started collaging as an undergraduate at Harvard and has continued the process in his visual and his literary work ever since. Influenced by Kurt Schwitters, Joseph Cornell and, more directly, Joe Brainard, his work combines art-historical and contemporary pop culture references. In May Ashbery received the Medal of Honor of the New York University's Center for French Civilization and Culture. In November he will be presented with the National Book Foundation's Medal for Distinguished Contribution to American Letters.

GRISELDA OHANNESSIAN, the former President and Publisher of the perennially exciting New Directions, died in August, after long years of Parkinson's disease. She devoted her working life to New Directions and was a fierce advocate of the press. Among authors she edited and encouraged were Lawrence Ferlinghetti, Antonio Tabucchi, Nina Berberova, Uwe Timm, Shusaku Endo, H.D., Elio Vittorini, Romain Gary, Henry Miller, Gert Hofmann, Stevie Smith, B.S. Johnson, Henry Green, William Saroyan, Mikhail Bulgakov and Raymond Queneau. She discovered H.E. Bates, James Munves, Henri Guiggonat, Carmel Bird and Christoph Bataille; and she mentored younger New Directions editors. Ohannessian also published a memoir, *Once: As it Was*, evoking in a wry, precise style her remarkable childhood: her father was Schuyler Jackson and her stepmother Laura (Riding) Jackson. Ohannessian's death sadly coincides with the 75th anniversary of New Directions, a milestone which is being celebrated with events across the United States, with Ferlinghetti reading with Michael McClure at San Francisco's legendary City Lights bookstore, Michael Palmer and Susan Howe in Boston, and Nicole Krauss, Anne Carson and Paul Auster at the historical Cooper Union in New York.

In their anniversary year New Directions garnered another Nobel Laureate. Swedish poet TOMAS TRANSTRÖMER was awarded the 2011 Nobel Prize for Literature in October. He has been on the list of possible recipients for twenty years, so the announcement is more a relief that justice has been done than a surprise. It would have been a surprise if Bob Dylan had received the award, a possibility widely canvassed at the last moment. Tranströmer's complete poems in English in one volume is entitled *The Great Enigma: New Collected Poems* (Bloodaxe is his British publisher). The best-known Scandinavian poet of the post-war period, Tranströmer is also the most widely translated. For many years seriously debilitated after a stroke, he continues to write. He is an avid pianist and has released a recording of classical piano pieces performed with his left hand. Though the largest, this is not the first award he has received; his honours include those almost inevitable preludes to the Nobel, the Neustadt International Prize for Literature, the Bonnier Award for Poetry, Germany's Petrarch Prize, the Bellman Prize, the Swedish Academy's Nordic Prize, the August Prize, and a Lifetime Recognition Award in 2007 from The Griffin Trust.

The Iowa Review has launched a remarkable dialogue among leading contemporary translators on the state of the art. Laurence Venuti, a *PNR* contributor and a translator from Italian, French and Catalan, throws down a very eloquent gauntlet. In his inaugural essay, *Towards a Translation Culture*, first conceived as a lecture delivered to the annual conference of the American Literary Translators' Association in October 2010, Venuti draws a bleak image of literary translators facing repeated rejections from commercially minded publishers. 'The occasional success of a contemporary foreign novelist like Roberto Bolaño or Stieg Larsson is misleading,' he asserts. 'The current situation has not really changed enough to indicate any across-the-board upsurge in sales of translations or any expansion of the readership for them.' He discusses the challenge of getting his translation of the contemporary Catalan poet Ernest Farrés published (eventually accepted by Carcanet, the award-winning, book-length *Edward Hopper*). *Iowa Review* editor Russell Valentino, head of the University of Iowa's Translation Workshop, has solicited answering essays from, among others, Tim Parks and Luise von Flotow. And there will be blood: Valentino quoted the *Review*'s onetime advisor Cole Swensen's observation that translation can often seem a 'blood sport', adding that 'we ask only that swords remain sheathed. Well, the dullest ones anyway, as they tend to make the greatest mess. Otherwise, have at it.' Members of the literary and translation communities are invited to join the conversation at www.iowareview.org.

The second International Translation Day took place at the Free Word Centre in London in September. Hosted by English PEN and Free Word in association with the London Book Fair's Literary Translation Centre, the symposium brought together translators, academics, teachers, agents, publishers, booksellers, funders, journalists and NGOs to discuss the state of the 'translation sector' and to propose solutions to the challenges it currently faces. Issues discussed included ways of popularising literature in translation; what we can learn from the success of other art forms such as music; the role of schools and universities in producing future translators; supporting the translation of minority languages; and the power of literary festivals. Read the ensuing report at www.englishpen.org. To find out more about English PEN's Writers in Translation programme or to contribute to the project, contact Emma Cleave, Programme Manager, at emma@englishpen.org.

Copyright © Michael Augustin 2011

English PEN reported that the Burmese poet ZARGANAR was released on 12 October as part of an amnesty for some 2,000 political prisoners. Zarganar (Maung Thura) was handed a 59-year sentence in 2008 after criticising the Burmese junta's poor aid response after Cyclone Nargis. English PEN campaigned relentlessly for his release, with a rally in Trafalgar Square and 'poetry protests' at the Burmese Embassy in London. The organisation sent thousands of letters and cards to Zarganar during his imprisonment. PEN co-hosted the first Burmese Arts Festival in 2010, at which Zarganar's work was featured. In 2009 the inaugural PEN Pinter Prize for an International Writer of Courage was awarded to Zarganar by Tony Harrison.

In a double celebration, glasses were raised to the 200th issue of *PN Review* at the vibrant Cartoon Museum in Bloomsbury, London, on the evening of 12 September, and at the International Anthony Burgess Foundation in Manchester on 8 September 2011. At the London event, the Lady Gavron, Carcanet's and *PN Review*'s Chairman, spoke about the place and purpose of the magazine; Michael Schmidt issued a roll call of thanks and spoke of the duty of resistance that falls to any independent literary magazine. There were brief and eloquent readings by two long-time contributors, Stanley Moss and Marilyn Hacker, and three more recent arrivals, poets Oli Hazzard, Will Eaves and Tara Bergin. It was a memorable evening which the *Economist* celebrated on its blog. 'The cartoons,' Schmidt commented, 'from Hogarth to Marc [not forgetting the Museum's brilliant current exhibition *Doctor Who in Comics 1964–2011*], kept the celebrations firmly grounded in the real social and natural world where poetry, however high it climbs, is always rooted.' The Manchester celebration included a lecture by poet, *PNR* contributor and Booker-longlisted novelist Patrick McGuiness on Donald Davie, who for some years co-edited the magazine with C.H. Sisson and Michael Schmidt, and a New Editors' Forum featuring Carol Rumens (*Guardian*), Rory Waterman (*New Walk* magazine), James Byrne (*The Wolf*) and John McAuliffe (*The Manchester Review*). The Arts Council's Alison Boyle welcomed the work of *PN Review* and spoke about the Arts Council's place in the straitened, challenging world of independent literary journals. Subscribers can access the full archive of the magazine at www.pnreview.co.uk.

The Jury of the Laudomia Bonanni International Award has given its 2011 prize to Irish poet JOHN F. DEANE. The eponymous award is in memory of an Italian writer born in 1907 in L'Aquila who achieved international renown as a children's author and essayist. The beautiful medieval town of L'Aquila in central Italy is the capital of the Abruzzo (the country of Gabriele D'Annunzio), a region severely damaged by earthquake in 2009. The award consists of a generous purse and a visit to L'Aquila for the presentation. Previous recipients include the Arabic poet Adonis, Derek Walcott, Yevgeny Yevtushenko, Edoardo Sanguineti and the Japanese writer Takano. John F. Deane's most recent poetry collection is *Eye of the Hare* (Carcanet, 2011).

Everything is going KAY RYAN's way these days. And she is coming our way. The popular and distinctive American poet, whose selected and new poems *Odd Blocks* has just been published by Carcanet, received one of this year's MacArthur Fellowships (half a million dollars over five years). 'Independent from schools of poetry and literary fashion,' the citation says, 'her mode of expression is a disarmingly clear and accessible style, characterized by concision, rhyme, wordplay, and wit.' The former American laureate received the Pulitzer Prize for Poetry earlier this year. She is touring Britain in early November, with readings at the Aldeburgh Poetry Festival, London's Southbank Centre, Edinburgh's Scottish Poetry Library and elsewhere.

The poet, diarist and long-time *PNR* contributor R.F. LANGLEY was posthumously awarded the 2011 Forward Prize for Best Single Poem on 5 October (British National Poetry Day). Langley died in January this year at the age of 72. His widow Barbara accepted the prize on his behalf. His winning poem, 'To a Nightingale', was originally published in the *London Review of Books*; his poetry, including *Collected Poems* (2000) and his 2007 collection, *The Face of It*, are published by Carcanet. The chairman of the judges Andrew Motion described the poem as 'a masterclass in precision'. Playing off Keats, it recounts an observational journey through nature: 'Red mites bowling / about on the baked lichen'; the 'Purring of two turtle doves'; 'Caterpillars which / curl up as questions marks'. Langley's friend J.H. Prynne read 'To a Nightingale' at his memorial.

Neil Powell remembers Herbert Lomas:
HERBERT LOMAS, who died on 9 September at the age of 87, was a more serious poet than he seemed and a finer one than his reputation suggests. His wartime university education at Liverpool was interrupted by three years in the army, mostly in India, after which he graduated with a First and an MA. He taught in Greece and, for ten years, at the University of Helsinki, before becoming Principal Lecturer at Borough Road College (now part of Brunel University). By then in his forties, he became a regular contributor of poems and reviews to Alan Ross's *London Magazine* and in 1969 he published his slender first collection, *Chimpanzees are Blameless Creatures*. Other more substantial books followed, including *Private and Confidential* (1974), *Fire in the Garden* (1984), *Trouble* (1992), *A Useless Passion* (1998) and *The Vale of Todmorden* (2003). The last two titles contain substantial sequences about his wartime experiences and about the Pennine town in which he grew up; a third sequence, 'Death of a Horsewoman', memorialises his wife Mary, who died after a riding accident in 1994. All these, together with unpublished work, were gathered into a handsome 400-page *Collected Poems*, called *A Casual Knack of Living* (Arc, 2009). He was also a prolific translator from the Finnish and the editor of *Contemporary Finnish Poetry* (1991).

I crossed swords with Bertie when he fiercely reviewed an early book of mine in the *London Magazine*: I wrote a spiky letter, he wrote a spiky reply. He was clearly a cussed sod, a kindred spirit: I knew we'd get on. So we did, when for ten years I lived near him in Aldeburgh, often meeting by chance on Crag Path or in the High Street. He looked like a pub man, but wasn't: his parents had kept one in Todmorden and it had put him off the places. Our last sustained encounter was at the grand annual lunch-and-reading of the Suffolk Poetry Society in 2006, he as chairman and I as a competition judge: it's the kind of occasion that can be tiresome, but Bertie – generous, funny and attentive to everyone – made it a pleasure. He liked 'lightness of touch', as he says in the Preface to *A Casual Knack of Living*. Casual or not, he had a knack of living, and he loved to share it.

Charles North remembers the American poet Paul Violi:
PAUL VIOLI (1944–2011), who brought an inventive wit, a sharp satirical spirit, and a variety of new forms to American poetry, died at 66 of cancer in April.

Violi grew up on Long Island, studied English literature and art history at Boston University, and upon graduating did map completion and survey work for the Peace Corps in Nigeria. Back in the US, he worked for WCBS TV and served as Managing Editor for *Architectural Forum* from 1972 to 1974. In 1970 he had begun to frequent The Poetry Project at St. Mark's Church-in-the-Bowery, becoming part of what came to be known as the Second Generation of New York School poets; in 1978 he was the Project's Interim Director. He also chaired the Museum of Modern Art Associate Council Poetry Committee. For the last three decades, Violi was a busy and popular university teacher. At the time of his illness, he was teaching in the graduate writing program at The New School and in the Department of English and Comparative Literature at Columbia University.

Comic lists drawn from everyday life were a Violi speciality: the call of a horse-race, a TV schedule, a 'Police Blotter', an index to an imaginary book. One of his best known poems, 'King Nasty', is a biting monologue in the form of a 'movie treatment' for an execution during the Reign of Terror. He also wrote in a lyrical vein. As difficult as it is to be taken seriously as a comic poet, Violi achieved that. His readings drew enthusiastic audiences in the US and UK. He received the Morton Dauwen Zabel Award from the American Academy of Arts and Letters, two National Endowment for the Arts Fellowships, the John Ciardi Lifetime Achievement Award in Poetry and a Foundation for Contemporary Arts grant.

LETTER

Poetry and Motions

Sir:
I have just perused your editorial in *PNR* 201 and, if my memory is not playing me false, I think you were briefly a member of the General Council of the Poetry Society in the 1970s. Of course, as you delicately hint, the current row was brought on by disagreements over *Poetry Review*, as were the rows in 1949 and in 1976. All of them resulted in the membership or factions of the membership seeking a coup, the most successful being the first when Muriel Spark was summarily dismissed as editor of *Poetry Review* following a putsch led by Dr Marie Stopes, whose poetry I do not know, but whose other work I am acquainted with after finding a manual on intimacy with one's partner in my paternal grandfather's effects after his death. Dr Stopes was subsequently on the General Council, briefly making a final appearance at the AGM in May 1950. The Report of the AGM in the July–August 1950 issue of *Poetry Review* records that she 'spoke to her motions', but on being overruled on the second, when she attempted to amend her motion without the requisite twenty-eight days' notice, she left the meeting, so that she could not speak on her third. All her motions were eminently sensible and were adopted in some form later, but by all accounts she was overbearing and bossy and had made enemies. Her exit foreshadowed the exits of the British Poetry Revival Group on the General Council in 1976, when they made what they thought was a strategic withdrawal, and the shambolic resignations of the current Trustees. Like Dr Stopes, they discovered nobody wished their return.

I attended performances of Bob Cobbing from the British Poetry Revival when he was alive and have had the privilege of reading the work of Alan Jenkins, who was one of the Trustees who resigned in the latest teapot tempest, but I have yet to find a parallel in their work with that of Dr Stopes. Perhaps, if I place recordings of Cobbing's explorations of the roots of language and Jenkins' ruminations on social mores at the end of the twentieth century in a box with the more perfervid of the love letters I received from the *amoureuses* of my youth and one or two extremely private trinkets, my appalled grandchildren will draw wholly misleading conclusions.

SILAS GUNN
By email

PNR

'It is, today, the most incisive voice of a vision of poetry and the arts as central to national life'
George Steiner

There is much to entertain and engage: reviews, poems, interviews, reports, news and letters.

PN Review invites readers to travel the world of poetry without passports, using the common currency of English. Poems, translation, essays and reviews alert readers and writers to developments at home and abroad, to work from the past, and to the promise and actual achievement of new writing.

PN Review is published six times a year and is available by subscription or from all good bookstores. Subscription is £36 for individuals and from £43 for institutions. All subscribers have access to PNReview Online.

www.pnreview.co.uk
The new **PN Review Online** will go live later this year. The site is now a rich and diverse resource for lovers of poetry and literature around the world. As each new issue is uploaded, a past issue is also added to the site. There is a powerful search engine which allows browsers to search by author, keyword, book title and reviewer, allowing access to decades of interviews, poetry, reviews and article from a range of the finest writers in the English language at the click of a mouse.

Subscription to this site costs the same as the paper magazine, starting at £36 per annum for individual membership, and is included in the magazine subscription rates.

NEIL POWELL
Rewards of Failure

The cartoonist Mel Calman used to draw, with very few lines, a recurrent character: a melancholic yet resigned fellow, typically to be seen sitting at his desk and thinking (in the bubble caption) some wryly incontrovertible truth. One of these read: 'Being a failure isn't as easy as it looks.' This seems neatly to suggest why unsuccessful people are on the whole more interesting and agreeable than successful ones; for success can come altogether too easily, while failure is usually hard work. Since the 1970s, success and failure have been defined almost exclusively in terms of wealth and possessions, but those of us who grew up a little earlier – children of rationing and shortages – may take a rather different view. We greatly resent having occasionally to spend money on replacing worn-out machines with new ones which seem both unnecessarily complex and mysteriously inferior; we actually *like* making do. Appalled and slightly baffled by the recent sight of looters making off with boxes of pointless electronic gadgets from shops and warehouses, I found myself reflecting that I've never possessed a freezer or a microwave, a digital or flat-screen television, a mobile phone or an iPod, and I've had my blue-humbug-shaped iMac for a decade now. That, however, is a stripling. My hi-fi system is over forty years old, the Rogers valve amplifier and the Celestion speakers as good as new, although the Garrard turntable's got a bit rusty from living in damp houses: these old things endure, while the twenty-year-old CD player already seems doddery. To many younger people – and here the heartless winners of the late capitalist world would be in complete accord with the desperate losers – this must all seem laughable and pathetic. And there may be little point in trying to describe to them the incomparable pleasures of failure: the weird notion that there might be greater, and cheaper, delights to be found in a second-hand bookshop, a junk shop or a village hall sale than in even the glitziest shopping mall.

I don't for a moment think there's anything especially virtuous in my position: it simply goes with a certain habit of mind, which in turn has much to do with a particular time and place. In truth, I began my apprenticeship in failure at the earliest possible moment, by apparently not much wanting to be born: the forceps left marks visible to this day. My reluctant arrival took place in East Sheen, but my parents soon decided to move out of London to a shoe-box cottage in rural Surrey. There was no mains drainage or electricity: we had a petrol-driven generator in the garage which my father liked to say went *chuggy-chuggy-chug-chug*, although quite often it didn't, which is why I learnt to read by the pure light of an opal glass shaded Aladdin paraffin lamp. Hot water came, of course, from an Ascot, and we also had a cube-shaped Ascot gas fridge. In the back garden lurked a concrete cesspool which had usually acquired a perceptible degree of ponginess by the time a dull green tanker from Dorking & Horley Rural District Council came to empty it. Once my father had left for work, driving to the station in his pre-war Rover, we were pretty much stranded – my mother and I, Bruce the labrador and Simon the tabby – until he arrived home in the evening. But most things came to Deanoak Lane: milk from the dairy in Charlwood, bread from the village baker in Leigh, groceries from the Norwood Hill Stores. Once a week, my mother would put on her special telephoning voice – 'This is Mrs Powell, from Rowbarns Cottage, phoning through the order' – and a man in a beige overall would duly appear with a box, to be unpacked (and the items ticked off on a list while he waited) on the little red formica-topped kitchen table, next to the mangle. On Saturday mornings, we'd make a grand expedition in the car to Reigate. There we divided, my mother going off to incomprehensible places such as butchers and fishmongers while my father and I together undertook more enjoyable forays: Westminster Wine and the tobacconist's for him, La Trobe's model railways and Mrs Lee's sweetshop for me. We'd eat cones of Forte's ice cream in the car or take jam doughnuts home for elevenses.

Life in Deanoak Lane taught me about improvisation and self-sufficiency – not bad formative skills for a writer – before I even went to school. I'd vanish for hours on end, across meadows and bluebell woods on foot with the dog, or along lanes and farmtracks on wheels: at first three, then two. The little glade at the bottom of the garden became an imaginary court; a pair of old garage doors were recycled into a makeshift den with rather surprising diamond-paned windows. In time, the den was replaced by a big timber shed ingeniously constructed by my father and furnished with serviceable oddments, in the spirit of *The Borrowers*, a book I loved. These came to include a tiny 'Bijou' typewriter, ancient but surprisingly sturdy, and a maroon, suitcase-shaped wind-up HMV gramophone; at weekends, I'd cycle off to jumble sales in neighbouring villages in search of 78s to play on it. Nothing plugged in because there was nowhere to plug it. I don't remember ever being bored.

But the habits I'd acquired, though they might be dignified by words such as resourcefulness and independence, wholly unfitted me for school. My first one was a kindergarten called High Trees (it now seems to be an old people's home, so perhaps I should return there for my second childhood) where everyone struck me as mad: I just couldn't connect with their shiny-gold-star view of things. My father or a neighbour would drop me off there on his way to work, but I had to catch the bus back on my own: that was the best bit of the day. Mother, dog and tricycle would meet me at the end of Deanoak Lane until I was old enough to leave my bike there, hidden beside a farm entrance, to retrieve on the way home. I'm not sure I learnt anything at High Trees: it certainly didn't prepare me for what came next, which was St Mary's in Reigate. This was a peculiar day prep school, adjacent to the grim barracks of Reigate Grammar School, of which it had once been part: the general idea was that if you went there you'd have a decent chance of going on to the 'grammar' at eleven, though that didn't take account of my increasing expertise in failure. I greatly disliked being middling, from which it seemed to follow that if I couldn't be excellent at something (and the field for this was limited) I should instead be spectacularly bad at it and, moreover, treat it with obvious contempt. Sometimes this didn't matter too much. I remember the day a bunch of us were herded off for a Cycling Proficiency Test, in some unholy place such as Merstham: by then, we'd moved to a house on the side of Colley Hill, outside Reigate, and there was nowhere within range I hadn't cycled – the only constraint usually being a parental hint that if I fulfilled some grand ambition I wouldn't be back for lunch or dinner or the start of next week – so going to Merstham to get a silly certificate shouldn't have been a bother. When I got there, it wasn't about cycling at all but about slowly navigating a line of traffic cones: not being much good at that, I decided to knock over as many of them as I could instead and was sent home, a failure, in disgrace. 'Never mind, dear,' said my mother, in a moment of terrible incomprehension. 'I don't mind,' I said. 'I'd have *minded* passing the stupid thing.'

Sometimes, though, it did matter. I could see that a failure to understand either maths or geography, for instance, might have more serious consequences than an urge to up-end traffic cones; but there was no help for it, especially as Mr Salmond, who taught both subjects, could be prompted to bristling and vastly entertaining rages, during which he spanked boys he especially fancied while the rest of us chortled smugly. On the other hand, I began to be quite good at English, encouraged by the fact that it was taught by a quizzical hunched Welshman called Gadfan Morris, in whom I recognised a noble failure after my own heart, no doubt a haunter of second-hand bookshops and definitely (though he never said a word about it) the author of radio plays broadcast by the BBC. Meanwhile, the headmaster, the Reverend Hobson, mysteriously taught us all Latin, a subject in which, at the age of ten or so, I might have plausibly attempted an O Level but which hadn't anything much to do with passing the eleven-plus.

The possibility that Reigate Grammar School mightn't welcome me with open arms, while secretly delighting me (I liked the look of Reigate Priory, the secondary modern, nearer home and housed in a beautiful building by a lake), prompted my parents to draw up contingency plans. They entered me for the entrance exams at both Whitgift and Trinity in Croydon, which I gratefully failed. They took me off to a cathedral school in the west country where the interviewing headmaster asked me to remind him which university he had attended: I realised he was a pompous fool who wanted to see whether I'd read his prospectus, so I politely wondered if he was perhaps feeling unwell and wasn't offered a place. Meanwhile, I sat the eleven-plus exams – juxtaposed in memory with *Quatermass and the Pit*, the most exciting thing I'd ever seen on television – and naturally failed. Or so I thought, until I came across a file of correspondence preserved, with my school reports, by my father. In February 1959, Surrey County Council told him that I had 'not satisfied the Committee' in the first part of the examination and invited me to sit a second part in March; in April, they wrote identically about the second part and asked me to attend an interview; in June they decided that I was after all suitable 'for grammar education', but didn't say where; it wasn't until late July that they wrote again to offer me a place at Horley County Secondary School, which was eight miles away and didn't sound much like a 'grammar'. My father frostily replied that he had 'felt it necessary to make other arrangements for my son's education'. Only now does it dawn on me that someone in the Education Department probably hadn't updated a card index and so thought that we still lived out at Leigh, for which Horley would indeed have provided the nearest secondary school.

Also in that file is a letter of 15 May 1959 from L.C. Taylor, the Headmaster of Sevenoaks School, confirming that I'd passed their entrance examination and been offered a place. I know why I passed: the appalling Hobson had told my parents that he thought Sevenoaks was too ambitious for me and a bit unconventional or even (he'd have sniffed) 'progressive'. I'll show him, I thought. Better still, there was an interview, which turned out to be with the genial, astonishingly young headmaster and a bearded chap, whom I'd soon be able to name as Brian Townend, classicist, jazz buff and brilliant boogie pianist. They somehow seemed to like a boy who walked and read and wrote and who cycled to village jumble sales in search of rare 78s, including, as luck would have it, early recordings by Louis Armstrong and Fletcher Henderson. As I was leaving, one of them said that they hoped they'd be seeing me again in September. They *what*? 'How did it go?' my father asked. He'd taken a day off work and was waiting for me in the car. 'Oh, you know, not too bad,' I said, with a giveaway grin. Not having lived a parallel life, I can't be certain that it was the right decision; but it was the right kind of decision, and that's what matters most.

SAM ADAMS
Letter from Wales

Recently (in *PNR* 200), I quoted from a letter David Jones wrote to *The Times* in June 1958 concerning the Welsh language. The loss of Welsh, he said, would impoverish England, 'for the survival of something which has an unbroken tradition in this island since the sixth century, and which embodies deposits far older still, cannot be regarded as a matter of indifference by any person claiming to care for the things of this island. It is by no means a matter for the Welsh only, but concerns all, because the complex and involved heritage of Britain is a shared inheritance which can, in very devious ways, enrich us all'. Worthy of repetition as it is, I would not so soon have brought it up again if I had not come across a very similar statement from an unexpected source: 'Welsh is of this soil, this island, the senior language of the men of Britain; and Welsh is beautiful… It is the native language to which in unexplored desire we should still go home.' These are the words not of a Welshman, nor of someone, like David Jones, consciously half-Welsh though born a Londoner. They were spoken at a public lecture in Oxford in 1925 by one who considered himself not simply English, but Mercian (which I have now learned means 'of the March'), or better still, Hwiccian, that is, belonging to a kingdom corresponding roughly to modern Worcestershire, Gloucestershire and part of Warwickshire, which was annexed by Mercia in the eighth century.

That, perhaps, gives the game away. They are the words of J.R.R. Tolkien, whose *Lord of the Rings* I have not read, but whom I felt I knew well as co-editor (with E.V. Gordon) of the OUP *Sir Gawain and the Green Knight*, first published in the same year as that Oxford lecture. My heavily annotated copy is a sixth edition, 1952. Faced with it as a set book in the honours course at Aberystwyth, I cannot pretend I was initially overjoyed, but I soon learned to savour it and am now immensely pleased and grateful that I once read, from beginning to end, a magical poem in its original fourteenth-century Lancashire English.

Tolkien's devotion to 'beautiful' Welsh, the confession of a philologist, was not idly expressed. As professor at Leeds and, later, Oxford, he introduced a mediaeval Welsh option into the Anglo-Saxon syllabus. He found an academic soulmate in Gwyn Jones, professor at Aberystwyth. They shared a professional interest in Old and Middle English and were both, also, writers of short stories and novels. He introduced Gwyn as a friend at a meeting of the Inklings, where, according to W.H. Lewis, brother of C.S., 'he turned out to be capital value; he read a Welsh tale of his own writing, a bawdy humorous thing told in a rich polished style which impressed me more than any new work I have come across for a long time'. Ah, I can just hear the smile in Gwyn's voice. The friendship led to the publication of Tolkien's long poem 'The Lay of Aotrou and Itroun', a tale of mediaeval Brittany, in Gwyn's magazine

The Welsh Review in December 1945.

I owe much of the above to Carl Phelpstead's absorbing *Tolkien and Wales: Language, Literature and Identity* (University of Wales Press, 2011). It tells us a great deal about Tolkien as a philologist, and as a writer, and suggests how the fantastical inspirations of the latter grew out of the former. One of the prime motives for his fictions was the desire, or need, to create a race of beings who would speak the languages he invented. The process of invention was not merely lexical, but concerned the fundamentals of language structure, such as syntax and the formation of the plural. It was essential, furthermore, that the language had its own linguistic history and the rich patina of legends that living languages possess, and that manufactured (in Tolkien's terms 'dead') systems, like Esperanto, do not. We learn (via Phelpstead) from Tolkien's letters that the Elvish language Sindarin, in *The Lord of the Rings*, was 'constructed deliberately to resemble Welsh phonologically'. But that was not enough. It also has 'a relation to High-elven [Quenya] similar to that existing between British (properly so called, sc. the Celtic languages spoken in this island at the time of the Roman invasion) and Latin'.

Few of us appreciate the value of learning another language to facilitate communication abroad, far less as the key to the door of another culture. That 'everyone' speaks English is an excuse for not bothering to learn another language. To Tolkien, however, language acquisition was an aesthetic experience, and he profoundly disagreed with those who would promote English as a world language. That was, he wrote in 1925, 'the most idiotic and suicidal [notion] that a language could entertain. Literature shrivels in a universal language, and an uprooted language rots before it dies'. He asked us 'to realise the magnitude of the loss to humanity that the world-dominance of any one language now spoken would entail: no language has ever possessed but a small fraction of the varied excellences of human speech, and each language presents a different vision of life'. If we this side of the March remember that Welsh is beautiful and do all in our power to treasure and preserve it, will the English on their side do so too?

Tolkien thought the greatest of all surviving works in Old English, the epic poem *Beowulf*, more typically Celtic than most things he had met written in a Celtic language. This took me back to Gwyn Jones's teaching of *Beowulf*. In our two-hour-long sessions, severe concentration on the text was leavened with anecdotes concerning matters Scandinavian or Icelandic. Along one of these byways I first heard that well-preserved bodies of Iron Age people turned up in peat bogs in Denmark. In the early 1970s I read P.V. Glob's *The Bog People* (Faber, 1969) where I learned that, along with men and women, artefacts were sacrificially deposited, most notably the Gundestrup Cauldron, a great silver bowl found by peat-cutters in the Raeve Bog, Himmerland, in 1891. It had been separated into sections before deposition, but re-formed is 42 centimetres high, has a diameter of 69 centimetres at the top and weighs almost nine kilograms. Experts still dispute where and by whom it was made, but it is broadly agreed that its repoussé decoration, inside and out, is characteristically Celtic.

In an exquisitely illustrated scene a line of warriors, on foot, is approaching a cauldron, over which one is suspended head first by a far larger figure. He is being sacrificed: a dog, signifying death, precedes those waiting their turn. Above the foot soldiers, a line of cavalry moves briskly away. While illustrations of the cauldron and Glob's explanation of them were still fresh in my mind, I happened upon Robert Graves' Penguin *Greek Myths*, where, in the introduction, I read, 'If some myths are baffling at first sight, this is often because the mythographer has accidentally or deliberately misinterpreted a sacred picture or dramatic rite'. I was reminded of the strange tale that begins the second branch of *The Mabinogion*. Matholwch, King of Ireland, visits Bendigeidfran, King of the Island of the Mighty, to receive the host's sister, Branwen, as wife. Efnysien, resentful brother of Bendigeidfran and Branwen, maims Matholwch's horses, and when Bendigeidfran hears of this insult, he gives his guest not only a fresh horse for each one maimed but also a magic cauldron that has the power to return to life men killed in battle, in Welsh called *pair dadeni*, 'cauldron of rebirth'. I was at once convinced that the original Welsh storyteller had seen the Gundestrup Cauldron, and in his narrative 'misinterpreted' the image described above so that its cauldron represents not sacrificial death but resurrection.

This minor revelation occurred almost forty years ago. I was so enthused that I wrote to A.O.H. Jarman, Professor of Welsh in Cardiff and far-famed Arthurian scholar, and laid the theory before him. With courteous academic coolness he dismissed my brainwave, and I put it aside. It is a little gratifying to find a note in Sioned Davies's excellent translation of *The Mabinogion* (Oxford, 2007) informing readers that 'Parallels have been drawn between this Cauldron of Rebirth and a scene portrayed on the Gundestrup Cauldron'. Without claiming proprietorial rights over those of Denmark, I think we ought to have a copy of that wonderful object in the National Museum at Cardiff.

As I write, the aftermath of the riots in England fills the media. Some commentators have reminded us that summer is the favoured time for rioting; others mentioned the possibility of a role for soldiers in keeping the peace and as quickly dismissed the idea. Untypically, the Tonypandy Riots occurred in November 1910. The unrest had begun in September that year when coal owners locked out the work force, with whom they were in dispute over miners' demands for a pay increase to take account of working in geologically difficult conditions, where much of their labour was unproductive, and therefore unpaid. At the height of the conflict on the streets soldiers were called in, and stayed. The strike continued until October 1911, when imminent starvation forced the men back to work. Everyone knows about the Tonypandy Riots, the last time, I thought, soldiers were deployed in a situation of that kind. I was wrong.

A hundred years ago to the day, 19 August 1911, during one of the hottest summers on record (124 degrees Fahrenheit was recorded in Cardiff in July), railway workers rioted in Llanelli. A national strike over pay had been called on 17 August and the strikers in Llanelli, their numbers swelled by sympathetic tinplate workers and miners, were intent on stopping rail traffic through the town. The press had vilified the strikers, who were among the poorest paid of British workers, and spread rumours that foreign agents were fomenting trouble. At the instruction of Home Secretary Winston Churchill, soldiers of the Royal Worcestershire Regiment were already in place, and when pickets stopped a train their commanding officer ordered a magistrate to read the Riot Act. This did not disperse the crowd and after a minute's warning the soldiers opened fire. Two bystanders, John John and Leonard Worsell, were killed and two others seriously wounded. This was the last time that British soldiers on mainland Britain fired on civilians. The event was commemorated in July on BBC TV's *One Show* and within the last week by media in

Wales and socialist organisations here and elsewhere. But it has been expunged from the history of the Royal Worcestershire Regiment, and London newspapers and broadcasters, if they ever knew, prefer to ignore it. So far as I am aware, there has been no word from David Starkey – surely an opportunity missed.

SIMON ECKETT

Keep on Truckin: Kitaj in the Lake District

While painting *The Rise of Fascism* (1975–79), R.B. Kitaj wrote to the publisher, poet and hiker, Jonathan Williams, 'Keep on Truckin. you are one of the only ones. In your own time, the daily thing may feel bleak but it is probably not and will look good when people look at your work and your days from outside.' For Kitaj 'the daily thing' became really bleak in 1994 when his wife Sandra Fisher died and his Tate Gallery retrospective received such criticism that after thirty-five years of living in England he left for his native America. Once *home* he engaged intensely with his American and Jewish identity, the death of his wife and his continuing anger at the critics. He died on 21 October 2007 at the age of seventy-four.

Now in 2011 Abot Hall Art Gallery, a Grade I listed Georgian house on the right bank of the river Kent in Kendal, Cumbria, offers us the opportunity to look at Kitaj's work and his days 'from outside'. The first major exhibition in England since the dark days of 1994, *Kitaj: Portraits and Reflections* displays Kitaj's versatility in oil, pastel, charcoal and screen-print and his voracious appetite for human engagement in art, literature and thought, for culture in its broadest sense, from his first paintings in the late 1950s to his last oils painted a few months before his death. As the curator and close friend of Kitaj's, Marilyn McCully, said in her speech opening the show, 'Michael [Raeburn] and I want to show Kitaj as a working artist, to re-introduce him to a new generation of art lovers.' They manifestly succeed in the intimate rooms of Abot Hall's upstairs galleries, but what they also lay bare through their picture hang is Kitaj's polarity, his swings through sympathy and love to edginess and anger, his fall into complexity and self-doubt.

The love is deeply felt. Take the graceful contours of Kitaj's 1978 charcoal *Lem (Sant Feliu)*, his son in profile sitting in a rocking chair reading a book. Or his screen-print portrait *For Love (Robert Creeley)*, the poet and close friend in burning reds and oranges caught face-on glancing downwards. It hangs next to the 1968 screen-print portrait *Star Betelgeuse* of the visionary poet Robert Duncan and the painter Jess, with whom Kitaj enjoyed staying when he visited San Francisco. But then comes the edginess, the dissonance, that sense of loss and thrown-togetherness of *Cecil Court: London WC2 (The Refugees)* of 1983–84, figures floating insubstantial, swinging like puppets through squares of harsh yellows, strokes of bright reds and dirty greens. Or the curators' pairing of the *Murder of Rosa Luxemburg* of 1960, slashes of red-black oil, with the blue-purple-black of *The Rise of Fascism*, a naked girl (Kitaj's future wife?) caught from behind cocking her right leg, 'heightening the sense of unease, lack of communication and sexual provocation'. Existential sadness and despair mask the cut-out faces in Kitaj's complex 26-colour screen-print, *Addled Art: Minor Works Volume VI* (1975), a look back at the early *Erasmus Variations* of 1958, also in the exhibition – 'the first modern art I committed', as Kitaj wrote in the catalogue of his 1994 Retrospective at the Tate.

Prowling from room to room, picture to picture, there's a feeling of a man on the hunt, of an artist in search of an answer. The visceral rawness and vulnerability, his leap from idea to intuition to misunderstanding, to experimenting with the surface of painting ('Arranging a life of forms on a surface will always be the bread and butter of picture-making'), transform the twists and turns of his ideas and pursuits into highly charged provocative images. In *Self-Portrait: Hockney Pillow* of 1993–94 Kitaj portrays the artist as harrowed figure, wrapped tight in a straitjacket of sheets and blankets. You sense the despair, that there's no truth to explain, no reason found for existence. But he's restless and wrestling and will continue to hunt through his powerful pastel and charcoal portraits of Richard Wagner (that glint of hatred), of Ludwig Wittgenstein and Sigmund Freud (palm clicking a pen, or is it a needle?), and in his writings and interviews. That need to explain, to interpret, to gloss and emend, in a torrent of words and suggestions:

My Jewish library is the heart of my house. This heart beats into my Yellow Studio in the garden, where I paint, and into a Drawing Studio… I made the Cézanne room because he teaches me lessons each day… Painters have always treated their last houses, or rooms (as in Mondrian's room) seriously: Monet at Giverny, Munch at Ekeley, Bonnard at Le Cannet, Auerbach at 2 The Studios, Kitaj at Westwest…

It's what makes Kitaj so compelling an artist. That he never stopped, that he Kept on Truckin right to the end.

JOHN GREENING

Nicholson, Suddenly

Norman Nicholson, who died almost twenty-five years ago, used to be widely read. He was a Faber poet. He won prizes, edited anthologies, had verse dramas performed, appeared on the A-level syllabus and was one of the featured writers in the American series Twayne's English Authors. He received a Cholmondeley Award the same year as Seamus Heaney. Heaney is, of course, from another generation (born, indeed, twenty-five years later, also at the outbreak of a world war) but it is hard to think that he could ever suffer the same degree of neglect. When Derry sings of a working-class childhood, of troubled landscapes, of spiritual longing, everyone listens. Why did we stop listening to Millom?

This was the English poet's omphalos: an agglomeration of iron and steel and slag, tucked away from the through-routes on the coast south of Whitehaven: an area overlooked by visitors to the Lakes, and generally unnoticed until the taxi-driver Derek Bird went berserk amongst its Viking remains in 2010. Nicholson was born in Millom in 1914 and remained there, in the same terraced house, all his life. His mother died in the flu epidemic when he was very small, and he was brought up by his shopkeeper father and his second wife. They lived above the outfitter's shop, their existence strictly tailored to the needs of a community for which the chief preoccupation was making ends meet and where any spare time involved church or chapel. The neighbouring Lake District was considered as exotic as the Mediterranean by the people of Millom (and most were too hard-pressed to visit it anyway), but it might be thought an advantage to grow up on the fringes of Wordsworth country, where there was already an acceptance that poets can matter – something rare on this side of the Irish Sea.

Nicholson tells the story of his childhood in his memoir, *Wednesday Early Closing* (recently reissued as a Faber Find), and what emerges is a voice whose innocence is perhaps the key to its endangered status. Interestingly, he first acquired a taste for poetry through his skill in recitation, and he made his name locally as a reliably entertaining performer before his father decided that he must 'cut out' such frivolities in favour of school work. But then tuberculosis struck (his stepmother's indifference to vegetables and snobbish resistance to anything home-made cannot have helped) and for a good many months young Nicholson could only whisper, and was confined to bed. He was never going to be striding the heights with Wordsworth; but by the time the Second World War had broken out, he had found a voice that the master might have recognised. And his debilitating condition would eventually prove one of his richest subjects (the title poem of *The Pot Geranium* for example, and later 'The Whisperer').

Nicholson claimed that his first true poem – and here's another link with Heaney – was about blackberries. It was included in his first collection, *Five Rivers* (1944), which is more characteristic of the period than of the author and reads as though it was designed to please Mr Eliot. There is an overtly religious note and more than a whiff of fashionable (if, considering the date, understandable) apocalypse, although the collection already shows the emerging loyalty to his home territory and his gift for industrial elegy. This continues in *Rock Face* (1948), where there is an increasingly literary dimension, too – poems on Cowper, Gray, Emily Brontë – and deeper experiment with allegory, notably in the gripping, if rather Eliotic, Duddon sequence, 'Across the Estuary':

It is not the eyes of the past
That stare through the mist,
But the eyes that belong to now.

It is not the faces of a dream
That bulge through the gloom,
But the faces of the waking sight.

It is not the voices of the dead
That leave the word unsaid,
But the voices of those who live.

What has not yet become audible is the Nicholson free verse line, the conversational tone, the witty deployment of what he calls 'the remark', which make his later volumes so delightfully idiosyncratic. Nicholson is essentially a happy, good-humoured poet, never more at ease than when picking some surprising memory of Millom life or folklore and elaborating on it. By the time he published *The Pot Geranium* in 1954, he had found a way of sounding like himself.

Nicholson prefaced his last and best collection with lines from Auden: 'A poet's hope: to be, / like some valley cheese, / local, but prized elsewhere'. The distinctive flavour of his mature voice came not just from the associations with West Cumbria – its stories, its characters, its imagery – but from his readiness to listen to what he heard there. In *Sea to the West* (1981) there is a bleaker scratching of pebble, glacier, scree, but in the 1950s he was beginning to tune in to something more comfortable, which he had been hearing all his life – the conversation around him:

'They dug ten streets from that there
                                         hole,' he said,
'Hard on five hundred houses.' He
                                                nodded
Down the set of the quarry and spat in
                                          the water
Making a moorhen cock her head
As if a fish had leaped. 'Half the new
                                                town
Came out of yonder...'
         (from 'Millom Old Quarry')

Such poems, opening with a casual 'remark', begin to be a recognisable feature of the Nicholson landscape, and it could be argued that they inclined to the formulaic in his last decades, so predictably do they end as they began. A local man who remarks 'I'm having five minutes' is a sonnet's length later 'Having five minutes to the end of time', and one who says 'It's late so soon' in the first line of 'Haytiming' is by the end repeating: 'That's the trouble with summer – / It's late so soon.' This is a trick learnt from Edward Thomas, of course, who in turn stole some moves from Wordsworth – the most important of which was to stop and listen to the beggar or leech-gatherer in the first place. And it is indicative of Nicholson's interest in cycles, too: how even things that seem to have escaped inevitably return. Particularly poignant is the last poem in his last book, which describes Halley's Comet, anticipating its arrival ('My father saw it back in 1910') as if it were one of the travelling salesmen who regularly called at 14, St George's Terrace:

And what of me,
Born four years too late?
Will I have breath to wait
Till the long-circuiting commercial
                                         traveller
Turns up at his due?
In 1986 aged seventy-two...?

In fact, the poet certainly had a chance to see the comet. He died in 1987, aged seventy-three, and is buried in Millom a few yards from the house where he was born and to which his orbit kept returning him.

Whether a voice like Norman Nicholson's can be properly appreciated today or has anything much to say to twenty-first-century readers is difficult to judge. The times that have changed seem to have left him stranded rather like the jellyfish that litter the shores of his beloved Duddon estuary. That his *Collected Poems* is now only available as a Faber Find (a digital print-on-demand service, or in Faber's words 'an imprint whose aim is to restore to print a wealth of lost classics') adds to this impression. Those same anecdotal pieces that felt refreshingly plainspoken in the sixties and seventies sound increasingly quaint, although 'Rising Five', for example, still appeals to all ages, and none of Nicholson's poems is less than entertaining. He never lost the old music-hall skills that he had perfected in the Methodist School Room in 1924. ('I did not want to be a solitary poet... I wanted an audience,' he wrote in his memoir. 'I wanted to make people listen.') In 'Nicholson, Suddenly', he recounts (with just the right degree of dead-pan and wryly rhymed amusement) how he came across the obituary of his 'other':

So Norman Nicholson is dead!
I saw him just three weeks ago
Standing outside a chemist's shop,
His smile alight, his cheeks aglow.
I'd never seen him looking finer:
'I can't complain at all,' he said,
'But for a touch of the old angina.'

Is this, then, the true Norman Nicholson? It has to be said that his main street and ironworks and estuary never quite achieve the mythological resonance of Heaney's well and pump and bog. Yet Nicholson in full, jaunty flow in a poem such as 'Weeds' is likely to prove perennial. And our particular age may well return to 'On the Closing of Millom Ironworks' ('whichever way it blows it's a cold wind now') or 'Windscale', which contemplates the after-effects of a nuclear leak, 'Where sewers flow with milk, and meat / Is carved up for the fire to eat / And children suffocate in God's fresh air'. Or it could be Norman Nicholson's late studies of beck and wall and dune and shingle and mountain, those striking short-lined pieces at the beginning of *Sea to the West*, that – by looking above and beyond Millom – keep their freshness for a new generation.

FRANK KUPPNER

Random Souvenirs of a Fleeting Return to the Continent

Very often, the mere fact that the author later died is itself already a sufficient comment on the absurdity of the eternalist pretensions inherent in his work.

There is something 'absolutely ultimate' which is going to be the right answer to one of our particularly inspired questions, is there, Dear Master?

The main problem surely is that practically everything, including thought – (including thought about transience!) – seems to be being produced on the assumption that these wonderful people here and hereabouts aren't really all going to die and go away completely.

(For which of us, tell me, has never really lived at the single most vital, most important moment of History? You, perhaps? Me?)

Or perhaps everything is fully intelligible only at ten past four in the morning?

In your ignorance, cretin, you thought the true number was a mere zero – whereas in fact it was an endless string of zeroes!

('But if I had known my life was going to be like this, Doctor, I'd have to have been somebody else already!')

I would be somebody else, but for the fact that, most unexpectedly, I turn out to be me. (And with this delightful sense of *failure* too!)

Oh, we would all like to be someone else, I dare say. But who?

No-one ever goes beyond himself. It is always still you, whatever it is.

A thing in itself? What thing? Do you mean that thing there? If not, what?

[The very notion of the thing-in-itself is a conceptual/linguistic trick of the light.]

How the Universe actually is, even now, is how the Universe is in itself.

As if, for instance, it could even be conceivable to know an apple *as it is in itself*. What apple?

Might it perhaps (really, as it were – somehow, deep down) be something else? Something else entirely? So – not an apple? What the human concept of X really is in itself! When no longer a human concept, apparently.

(To experience it as it would be if there were no experiencer there to experience it! And what could it possibly be *like* then?)

'What is ultimate reality?' Well, for that matter, what *isn't* ultimate reality? As far as I can make out – which I suppose need not be very far, I admit – there is *nothing but* ultimate reality.

The sense that something unutterably great is happening, my father always used to say, is nearly always an illusion.

(Oh, yes. That familiar, haunting pop-song from my youth. *My Old Man's A Continental Philosopher*. Already something of a contradiction in terms, is it not?)

Supernatural. Superficial. It all comes to much the same thing very soon indeed.

(The sense that something unutterably *un*important is happening is probably always an illusion too.)

Still, Dad. No doubt the Cosmos is something of a special case.

But, I suppose, in the end – (if that is quite the phrase) – your parents are merely the particular people who happened to produce you. (Yes; you. (Try to be good, by the way.))

So. I'm alive. Thou art alive too. How very surprising (all things considered). (Forgive me both my anachronisms. (Isn't the entire sentient Universe – (at least!) – rather an anachronism, by the way, Your Honour?)

As for 'going beyond oneself' – well – perhaps it's the sort of thing one can build up to gradually. First of all, say, bravely stretching a toe out beyond one's initial limits – and then, as it were, taking heart, and extending the foot even further. (Then maybe the other foot? And there, eventually, you are!)

'To become itself.' Such a reverberant turn of phrase! (Of course, at times one again rather fears that the entire Universe has somehow failed to become itself.) (My over-arching plan is – to become myself! Not a *grossly* hubristic project, one might at least suppose.)

Nothing is not the meaning of the Universe.

Nothing transcends the world.

(Or: There is nothing that transcends the world.)

Absolutely none of us can ever in any way get any deeper into it than the acutest actual human thinkers can manage, flaws and all. (*Higher Exam Question*: 'What does "It" in the previous sentence refer to, children?')

Nothing is not the meaning of the Universe.

(This means something quite different now of course.)

Careful, my child! Try to keep authentically close to Being as such! There's a good boy! (Er – good girl, sorry.)

Are we not nearly all, Sisyphus, more or less working non-stop doing our best to make sure we receive our invitation to a sublime unending final party which is in fact never even going to be given?

(But surely non-Being must itself also be the great non-problem?)

Hello there. I wish to penetrate deep into the nature of Being. (But first things first! Is there by any chance – erm – a, you know – a free toilet anywhere in this bloody place?)

It seems to me, Joseph, that just about anything could just about end at just about any point. No?

JANE YEH

Seven Poems

Yesterday,

The black cat that always sits on the bin next door wasn't sitting on the bin.
• The price of porcine commodities rose slightly, while that of the vegetarian English breakfast at my local café remained the same.
• No-one attempted to assassinate the French librarian at my old university, despite his insistence on labelling paperback books 'INFÉRIEUR'.
• The last of the flannelette pyjama tops I had stocked up on in America abruptly gave up the ghost.

Something was missing from my life (other than the black cat and pyjama tops).
• A new recycling regimen in my borough wasn't enough to make up for it.
• Neither were reports of recent advances in tooth-whitening, fuel injection, and women's rights in various countries.
• Nor did a certain Hollywood actor's growing resemblance to Mayor McCheese prove sufficiently distracting.

The shallowness of my existence was hardly a novel development.
• I had been known to frequent discount shopping outlets voluntarily and to reject suitors based solely on hair length.
• I spent hours devising ingenious interrogation tactics for Cluedo, despite having no-one to play with.
• I was a card-carrying member of a secret organisation devoted to the abolition of Velcro.

It was unclear to me whether literature could offer any salvation.
• Volatility in German type markets meant that italics were now *verboten*.
• The invention of see-through paper resulted in a move towards blatant transparency in fiction.
• A sort of massive rise in textual ambiguity rendered the love poem obsolete ... or did it?

Eventually I grew weary of thinking on these conundrums.
• The neighbour's hideous spaniel popped out for a moment and gave me a soulful look.
• The number of charitable donations to Battersea Dogs' Home I planned to make one day subsequently decreased to zero.
• Scientists declared there was a 60% chance that hell would freeze over due to climate change, while Streatham would remain unaffected.
• A level 5 pollen alert led to extreme hoovering, even inside my hermetically sealed castle.

The Birds

They pack up around three with their incessant chirping.
Their headgear includes goggles, stripes, crests, and masks.
They peck for a living for their grub, which sometimes includes grubs.
They snack on gingerbread and candy corn from off witches' houses.

On the ground they look helpless. Their hopping looks absurd.
Their tiny brains contain thoughts about worms; fluff; other birds; and goats.
(What kind of weird-ass animal has a beard but can be milked?)
They switch into defensive mode whenever a goat or person comes round.

Their brains are so small they forget how to fly until they do it.
If you make them cross, they'll poop on you.
If they see a witch they chirp, 'Witch!' and retreat to a safe distance.
(The witches want to bake them and use their feet for coathooks.)

Their nests may be built out of yarn and dental floss.
They keep spare nuts in select locales for future munches.
They pick on smaller birds to practice seeing off predators (like the witches).
They keep their eggs hidden in bushes, like jellybeans or spiders.

If you cross them, they'll pluck your eyes out.
Their heads are the size of dolls' heads, but their bodies don't fit into the clothes.
If they spy a goat they try to confuse it by flying backwards in slow-motion.
They want to live out in the open like people, but they can't be arsed to make weapons.

On Sorrow

This is as much space as I can spare to look at ferrets. My friend's ferret used to burrow into the red velvet cushions of her sofa, worm its way under the seats and into unretrievable nooks. Ferrets are mustelids, meaning their nearest relations are weasels. Take care! A pile of laundry might be hiding a napping ferret. My friend's ferret liked to crawl up the bootcut legs of her jeans while she was wearing them. Ferrets are crepuscular, which means they're most active at dusk and dawn. Some are adept at stealing small objects such as socks and unused tampons. My friend's ferret made a clucking sound whenever it was happy, like a sweet fur-covered baby. It would do a frantic hopping routine out of sheer excitement if you threw it a handful of soft balls (this is commonly known as the ferret war dance). One day her ferret just disappeared. It must've tunneled through a gap in the ash skirting boards of her study and landed in unknown territory. I like to think it found its way outside and survived, but equally it might be rotting in the wall. Sometimes a ferret is just a ferret, but my friend said it was as bad as losing a child. Ever since then we haven't seen each other much. The truth is most people can afford to lose something they love. (My friend, for instance, still had a partner, and later a baby and dog.) Ferrets have a distinctive musky scent, which some people find off-putting. The correct term for a group of them is a business of ferrets. Whenever I remember my friend's ferret, I think of its bright beady eyes.

The Big Sleep

I eyeballed an elaborate clock. The gun hung
Gaily in the pocket of my harlequin blazer, which matched
My argyle socks. The sky was like a sceptical grin
Or a self-reflection. I elbowed the dregs of the afternoon

And burst into the shindig. The whole gang was there:
Señor Oso, Monty the Skunk, Chip Butty, and some dames
Half-inching the cheesy nibbles. In the middle
Was the clever dick I'd come to see, my archrival

In gumshoeing. We bickered over who had the bigger
List of clients; Chip tossed me out. In the gutter
I rehashed why I'd gone in the first place to
That dive, the Croque Monsieur – the hollow-eyed

Mother, the missing girl, the trail of clues leading to
The shadowy capo of an underground doughnut ring,
The smell of leather, the severed hand, the murdering
Bastard who'd kill a kid for no reason – they all knew

Where to find him. I dusted off my Damascene holster
And went back in. The silence was almost existential
Until Herr Oso pulled out a gun and sneered,
'Time's up, you twerp.' Shots rang out. I saw red,

Like the red hair of the girl who'd died alone
In a cellar, like the red-rimmed eyes of her friends
At the funeral, like the blood-red stain spreading across
My shirt as I lay on the cold linoleum, having failed her –

While that dirtbag was still out there somehow,
Laughing. It wasn't fair. My life was oozing
From my side like melted cheese. My blood was pooling
Like a pancake on the checkerboard floor. When I saw

Monty grinning down at me, it finally clicked –
He was the joker behind it all. My last move
Was to reach into my comedy jacket and shoot.
It wouldn't bring her back, but it sure felt good.

Four Sisters: Sargent's The Daughters of Edward D. Boit

This poem won third prize in the 2011 Edwin Morgan Poetry Competition, and appeared on the competition website (http://edwin-morganpoetrycompetition.co.uk)

Each girl has got her best dress on.
At dawn, they were washed and brushed and tied
Into pinnies. Then the long wait

Until afternoon, when their florid mamma
Peers in for a moment; is off to the coiffeur's.
The one on the floor wants to know what her doll

Thinks about being painted. The one in the door just wants
To cut her hair short. The one on the side is trying
Her hardest not to fall over. The last one

Dreams herself into colour a limb at a time.
Her eyes look dubious. If the world
Makes us pay for our pleasure, how much will she owe?

Her aberrant shadow trails her like a servant.
Her beruffled wrists know no compulsion.
Her indolent sash is a cascading sigh.

She won't marry for love, or money.
She'll found a museum for unmanufacturable inventions.
She can't let them find out where, or why.

Sherlock Holmes on the Trail of the Abominable Snowman

This poem appeared on the website http://www.likestarlings.com

1. A wrong turnip (taken for a miscoloured swede)
2. The effortless spill of night, disrupted
3. Design for a semaphore temple in semi-Greek marble
4. Textbook occurrence of London rain: barely
5. Whipping up a dastard-and-goat soufflé

6. Time for acrobatic whitewashing of someone's back story
7. Settled how to prune the epistemological topiary
8. O tempura, O monkeys
9. Himalayan word for *mishegoss*, or a type of pasta
10. Behind the scenes at the prickly ambassador's ball

11. Shoeprint, fishwich, snowmelt, mismatch
12. Riding the rails to the lowlands for some jiggery-pokery
13. Who supplied the lurcher with the faulty parka?
14. Heavily under-represented in cliff-climbing circles
15. Make way for donkeys

16. The imperceptible wishbone of the evening dislocated by yowling
17. Off to hell by torchlight and celluloid sledge runners
18. A frozen crocus laid over a well-veiled crevasse
19. *Camera oblongata*
20. After the ice palace rope bridge two-yak standoff

21. Home: slice of flambéed haunch in philosophy sauce
22. Towards a general theory of plonk
23. Whispers (supermoon, theremin, Sasquatch, postman)
24. Cryptid or goose-chase as seen through branches
25. Uncertain outcomes predicted in the secret cattery

On Baseball

This poem appeared on the website http://www.likestarlings.com

My mechanics are almost entirely self-taught.
Hawking and strutting, I hit my spots.

Nobody talks to me, they are all afraid.

The nature of perfection is half fluke, half
Fiction, like the mighty appaloosa

That haunts the hometown lake. I'm from one of those states
That never got finished, that just sort of unravelled, like
                                                    the sound

Speed makes as it blows right past you.

*

I was a nibbler, a picker, a quitter, a rube, whatever
Happened to me happened. I had *no control*.

*

The nature of perfection is repetition. Repetition is
A kind of half-dream, half-living, a kind of curse

Like that guy who got chomped every day by a vulture
And just couldn't die. I can throw a hook

That'll swoop to the dirt and kiss you goodnight. I can pull
The trigger with a splitter, snap off a hard change,

Then put you away with a back-door slider.

Dog at my side, I hawk and strut
With pride. I know she loves me.

*

The ball sings a little when perfection is near. Back in the day
My life was one big cross-up. I don't know how I got here.

I kick my toe in the dirt, finger the ball like a prayer.
The lights get hotter. Nothing moves from its spot.

The nature of perfection is a paradox, because the minute
You start thinking about it it's gone.

THOMAS DAY

Variant Editions of Geoffrey Hill's Mercian Hymns

The text of Geoffrey Hill's *Mercian Hymns* reprinted in full in Hill's 2006 Penguin *Selected Poems* bears a strange unlikeness to the poem as it appears in the original André Deutsch pamphlet of 1971, and then again in *Somewhere Is Such a Kingdom: Poems 1952–1971* (Boston, 1975) and the Penguin *Collected Poems* of 1985. Where the earlier books exactly replicate the lineation of the original pamphlet, the 2006 version rejigs the text by packing in more words per line, thus altering the words that begin and/or end any given line, as well the spatial positioning of those in between. *Selected Poems* ostensibly observes the distinctive shape of *Mercian Hymns*' 'versets of rhythmical prose', as Hill characterised the form in his interview with John Haffenden:[1] short paragraphs justified at both margins, with the first line of each 'outdented', slightly overhanging the left margin – like the effigy on Offa's coins as described in hymn XIII, at once 'kempt and jutting'. But it's as if the liquid has set differently in the mould. So, to take an instance at random, the first lines of hymn XXIII in the original read

> In tapestries, in dreams, they gathered, as it was enacted, the return, the re-entry of transcendence into this sublunary world. […]

while *Selected Poems* has

> In tapestries, in dreams, they gathered, as it was enacted, the
> return, the re-entry of transcendence into this sublunary world. […]

This means that while the original verset runs to six (or five and a half) lines, concluding with 'master- / works of treacherous thread', the 2006 text falls just short of five. Similar anomalies run through all of the rest of the hymns.

A crucial distinction between poetry and prose, it could be argued, is that the latter lacks the precise spatial coordinates of the former. There isn't a meaningful discrepancy between, say, a large-print edition of *Pride and Prejudice* which cuts the first line off at 'It is a truth universally acknowl-', budging 'edged, that a single man in possession of a' down to the second and 'good fortune must be in want of a wife' onto the third, and an edition which fits the whole sentence onto one line, because in prose the sentence or clause is the unit of meaning, not the line. In poetry, most obviously perhaps in end-rhyming poetry, it clearly does matter that a certain word should appear at the end of a line and not at the beginning or in the middle of the next, or vice versa. A poem prompts the reader to make vertical and diagonal associations between words, as well as having to be read horizontally from left to right, and the spatial properties of a poem may often interfere with and modify its syntactic sense. In describing *Mercian Hymns* as 'versets of rhythmical prose' Hill was careful to distinguish the form from the prose poem; nevertheless, his phrase points to a peculiar combination of prose and verse elements, a combination which unsettles the (in)significance of word placement, line ending, and their potential alteration.

This is the first verset of the original hymn III:

> On the morning of the crowning we chorused our remission from school. It was like Easter: hankies and gift-mugs approved by his foreign gaze, the village-lintels curlered with paper flags.

Are these line endings are prosily arbitrary or poetically premeditated? There would be a case for thinking Hill means to make something out of 'mission', the word gaining a new lease of life from out of the sundered body of the old, like the Word, 'like Easter': sense 1 of the *OED* entry for 'mission' is 'In Trinitarian theology: the sending into the world of the Son or Spirit by the Father, or of the Spirit by the Son, esp. for the purpose of salvation'. But that leaves the conspicuously redundant 're-', which fails to live up its privileged placement as the first line's last word, being something less than a word. Last words acquire special significance in lines two and three from the internal punctuation, which builds them into enclosures of their own. Somewhat paradoxically though, the definite article that concludes the third denies the line definition as a line, the rhythm of the prose, which is also partly established by the preceding comma, asking us to proceed without pause to the important business of the clause. On the other hand again, taking an awkward break at the end of the line could have the effect of converting the prosier, short-vowel pronunciation of 'the' to a longer-vowelled 'th*ee*' – an apt aural emphasis for a so-called 'hymn'. One could even claim a rhyme between 're-' and 'the', the quatrain pattern completed by the semantic rhyming of 'hankies' and 'flags' as a mode of (pseudo-Christ-like) surrender. Yet any such claims are rendered academic by Hill's *Selected Poems*, in which the prose imperatives override those of a putative poetic form: the last words in each line in that edition are a restituted 'remission', 'gift-mugs', 'curlered', and, hoisted an inch or so to the left, 'flags'.

Or consider whether the past participle endings also function as line endings in the second verset of hymn XII.

> The men were paid to caulk water-pipes. They brewed and pissed amid splendour; their latrine seethed its estuary through nettles. They are scattered to your collations, moldywarp.

Two such adjacent endings could be coincidence, but three, one hazards, must be technique, although the third of those participles, 'scattered', brings into play a randomness that tells against the regimented look of the right hand margin. Moreover, the sense of an inner fluidity threatening to burst its seams (the implication seems to be that the men do not do what they are paid to do), and the piss – at variance with the formal-sounding 'latrine' – organically shaping its own winding course 'through the nettles', might point to a formal pliability that partially justifies the warping of the mould in *Selected Poems*. There are other moments which hint at a creative reciprocity between the two versions. In the previous hymn, in the lines 'Exactness of design was to deter imitation; mutil- / ation if that failed', the performative mangling of the line break seems very much part of the design. But this potentially gains an extra dimension from the paradoxical mutilation of 'mutil- / ation' in *Selected Poems*, the longer line re-fusing the severed particles. 'Exactness of design was to deter imitation', but it may be that the poem's design invites imitation too ('was to', like 'were paid to', implies thwarted intention). 'Seasons touched and retouch- / ed the soil', Hill writes in the subsequent verset, and maybe this too is a sign that his hymns aren't all that sacred, a recognition that it is natural for works of art to be 'retouched' (2006) over time.

Maybe, but *Selected Poems* remains vulnerable to imputations of casual editing. The author who, in his note to *The Mystery of the Charity of Charles Péguy* (1983), praises Péguy as 'A man of the most exact and exacting probity, accurate practicality, in personal and business relations, a meticulous reader of proof',[2] and who projects onto Offa 'a care for natural min- / utiae' (XIV) which in many respects he shares, appears on this occasion to have been more than a little careless in his proof-reading. Or else complacent enough to have delegated the task to minions; or, out of contempt for the unashamedly commercial motives that a *Selected Poems*, like those *Best of...* albums, might entail, to have averted his foreign gaze from the whole enterprise (though the approving authorial stamp seems to have been put on the American edition of *Selected Poems* published by Yale University Press in 2009, judging by the full-size mug-shot of him glaring out at nothing which adorns the front cover). Hill is, of course, capable of adopting self-parodic stances in these matters, most notably in *The Triumph of Love* (1998), in which the intrusions of an inept editor serve as a comic conceit. The 'comic sub-plot' of his seminal essay 'Poetry as "Menace" and "Atonement"', his contention that 'an anxiety about *faux pas*, the perpetration of "howlers", grammatical solecisms, misstatements of fact, misquotations, improper attributions' is a form of guilt that writers write in order to atone for – and that, in this connection, 'one of the indubitable signs of Simone Weil's greatness as an ethical writer' is 'that she associates the act of writing not with a generalized awareness of sin but with specific crime, and proposes a system whereby "anybody, no matter who, discovering an avoidable error in a printed text or radio broadcast, would be entitled to bring an action before [special] courts"' – , further positions Hill as a witness for his own prosecution.[3] His notes to *Mercian Hymns*, which, in another editorial howler, *Selected Poems* has entirely dispensed with, accordingly evince a wry embarrassment at the errors of his exacting ways: 'I seem', he confesses of his use of the word 'wire' in hymn XXV, 'not to have been strictly accurate', with something of Eliot's diffident scrupulosity in the spuriously scholarly 'Notes on *The Waste Land*' ('I am not familiar with the exact constitution of the Tarot pack of cards'; 'I do not know the origin of the ballad from which these lines are taken'). It would seem to be going too far, though, to see the not strictly accurate handling of the text's lineation half a lifetime later as part of an elaborate self-deprecating joke by the poet. For one is crossing a line that distinguishes the textual from the paratextual, the conceit from contingent circumstance: comfortable fictions become unruly realities; 'I seem' suddenly shades into 'I am'. Such boundary-blurring is very much the province of *Mercian Hymns*, which stages kinds of play that do go too far: 'The children' in hymn XIX who 'shriek / and scavenge, play havoc. They incinerate boxes / rags and old tyres'; the *Boy's Own* imagination of XXII ignited or incited by the wireless reports of actual war; Ceolred, 'sniggering / with fright' as Offa lures him 'down to the old quarries, and flay[s] / him' (VII); the 'laugh' juxtaposed with 'a cough' in II, the latter perhaps a cover for the *faux pas* of the former. Yet if the erroneous republication of *Mercian Hymns* is meant to be a private joke several degrees subtler, realer, and more perfectly imperfect than *The Triumph of Love*, then any laughter it elicits would have to be nervous indeed, since it would suppose Hill in possession of a level of creative foresight (one might think of it also as flaw-sight) that is, to remember Offa's self-estimation in hymn XXIX, staggering. And it's that same supposition, oddly, that confounds the element of joking, Offa's enormous self-estimation no longer a caricaturish exaggeration of Hill's own in thinking himself capable of alchemising gradual slippage in poetic form into formal sin – at once an enormous estimation of the reader who is to attend to such slow-burning sleight of hand.

Notes
1 John Haffenden, *Viewpoints: Poets in Conversation with John Haffenden* (London: Faber and Faber, 1981), pp. 76–99 (p. 93).
2 Geoffrey Hill, *Collected Poems* (Harmondsworth: Penguin, 1985), p. 206.
3 Geoffrey Hill, 'Poetry as "Menace" and "Atonement"', in *Collected Critical Writings* (Oxford: Oxford University Press, 2008), pp. 3–20 (pp. 15, 9, 9–10).

JEAN-PAUL DE DADELSEN

Three Poems

Translated by Marilyn Hacker

The Great Ledger

They'll tell you that sunshine will follow the rain; they'll tell you
That a bird in the hand is worth two in the bush.
    Don't believe it.
It is good that after the rain comes the deluge; it is excellent
That a bird in the hand brings two wolves out of the bushes; it is necessary
That for not having gone often enough to the well
    The pitcher be broken.

Erase and start again. They'll tell you that after two 9s there's often a 36
And that last summer at Evian zero came up three times in a row.
    It's true
A colonel who'd gone to the Ecole Polytechnique played the limit three times on zero;
Five hundred thousand francs; thank you from the employees, thank you sir from
The accountants of the great ledger where your military service record has always
    Been noted down.

Campaigns under Charles known as the Wise, under Pyrrhus, under Ramses II,
Under Hamurabi; nine wounds; two dead on the scaffold;
    A suicide;
A life wasted as a magistrate's wife. As decorations
A child raised to hate everyone, a word kept despite common sense,
Three defeats by stubbornness against all evidence,
    Dishonour and fidelity.

He says to her: So you stayed with him? Well, yes, she
Stayed with him; got laid three times, of which the first
    Was spoiled for her
And the third spoiled by him. But who knows on what grounds.
That was part of her own service record. And by what right
Did he feel himself so magnanimous, so generous, for having forgiven her?
    She belongs to no one.

I don't belong to myself. I don't know where I come from, I don't know
What is marked down in my favour or against me
    In the great account book.
I am not my forgetfulness I am not my laziness and am not
My sluggishness. But from the depths of my memory I am ashamed
I am ashamed I did not cry out against you
    Eternal One.

The Eternal is within me and watching me, more useless
Than a breeze's evening breath over water, calm
    And memoryless.
He watches from deepest within me my thoughts my graven images,
My puerile need for a God who has a given name
My demented desire for a woman who will love
    Only me.

The woman is wise. She never loves except across us, loves
The idiot, the pig and the coward hidden in us, loves only
    Our death

Which we hold as a plum holds its pit. Never keeps her word,
Never is surveyed or measured, gathers no moss, never
Fails to reward the fool who pretends to forget that she is
   Under orders.

The madam who knew that politeness is a form of charity
Will be the great-grandmother of a novelist with a rare
   Refinement of thought.
Each day Saint Louis' sperm flows like water
On the straw mattresses of Burgundy and southern Brittany.
Nothing has rhyme or reason, nothing is for our use.
   After us comes the sunshine.

South America, High Plateaus, Guitar

The undone tasks, they'll be done later.
In secret, night reopens the doors of an ancient country.
Guitar, that the hand strums, that the palm lightly
   strikes, that the finger
      plucks to make it briefly moan and
         resign itself.
   Guitar, deep well.
To the man who throws a pebble in, it answers
with the always-widening wave of melancholy.
Melancholy is not a complaint but a place.

   Did I say
the police who come for their bribes, the credit
and investment bank, the money lost throwing dice with
the son-of-a-whoring-bitch from the bus company,
the cornfields burned, the dead child? Did I cry out? Beg?
   I say night, I say the absence
of even a breeze in the trees sleeping dreamlessly

different, in that, from men, I say
the plucked string, that hollow slapped by the palm,
that moaning stopped, covered over by silence,
and just as when you plunge a net in a stream
so deep that it flows making no sound whatsoever,
the guitar to the brim and then
overflowing in muted waves, the guitar that is now
   filled up with night.

Lot's Wife

Serious Sodom boasted its budgets, its laws
For neither war nor prophecy had soiled the city.
Housewifely Sodom took care of its temples, its roofs
With a fortitude earned by not praying for rain
And remained unsullied by ecstasy, riot and hope.
Honest Sodom spreads its ramparts across the plain.

I was born in a country of rocks and springs, far from the plain
In a goiterous village of folk with no silos, no laws.
The cripple extends his cracked bowl, the idiot, grinning in
                            hope,
Sings and leaps under the mud shower skirting the cities.
Hunger comes with winter; feast days follow rain
And disguised as a sleepwalker, God sometimes walks on
                            the roofs.

The angel appeared as I languished one night on the roof
Who had come to save me from the savage city of the plain.
Now I return toward my homeland of stone and of rain.
He showed me the hidden door in the wall of their law.
On this path which rises above the city
I can smell on the wind the wide spaces of hope.

Don't turn back. Don't listen. Abandon all hope
Of rescuing even that deaf-mute child and that dog. The roofs
Seep beneath the foul cloud stagnating over the city.
But who am I to be saved alone on the plain?
An ass brays. A carter and his horse, knowing no law,
Return toward what they believe is a promise of rain.

The trees sleep dreamless, long deprived of rain.
The trees in the dimming light make signs without hope.
Dogs frolic. A cat gives birth. The law's
Base lava will wash over these roofs
And the fountains dimly humming on the plain.
Who am I to be saved in exchange for the loss of a city?

One God, true God, God of all the cities,
God who is prodigal with or who holds back rain,
God who exiled me long ago on the plain,
I do not want to survive without hope.
These harmless palm trees, unloved children, roofs
Undefended, all bear witness against your law.

Lot's wife, the foreigner, looks down at the roofs
Of all those loveless beings blinded on the plain
And resigned, descends to be lost with the city.

Jean-Paul de Dadelsen was born in Strasbourg in 1913, to a bilingual (German/French) family; his father was of Danish descent. After an *agrégation* in German literature in 1936, he joined de Gaulle's Free French Army in London during the war. Later, he became a journalist for Albert Camus' Résistance newspaper, *Combat*, and a close friend of Camus. After the war, he worked as a radio-journalist for the BBC's French Service. He did not begin writing poetry until his mid-thirties, and he died at forty-four of a brain tumour. Only a few poems had been published before his death. The majority of his work was published posthumously, edited by his friend François Duchêne at the request of his British widow, Barbara de Dadelsen.

   The poets Henri Thomas and Denis de Rougemont, among others, consider him to be the greatest Alsatian-French poet.

ROGER CALDWELL

'The Present King of France is Bald': On Possible Worlds

Leibniz once stated that 'many stories, especially those called novels, may be regarded as possible, even if they do not take place in this particular sequence of the world which God has chosen.' That is, God's world did not include Don Quixote, although it could have done; it only included a certain Cervantes who 'invented' him and his adventures – indeed, invented him so vividly that he 'lives' on in readers' heads to the present. Similarly, God's London did not include Sherlock Holmes or Mrs Dalloway, nor could they have met, say, on Regent Street or in Kensington Gardens – being fictional, they could not have met anyone anywhere, except in the pages of a novel. In Leibnizian terms, it was not in God's plan to instantiate or actualise Don Quixote or Sherlock Holmes or Mrs Dalloway: they are possible entities only, whereas we ourselves and all the people who have ever lived or will ever live are not only possible but were, are, or will be, also actual.

For Leibniz God was, amongst other things, a sort of master-logician: he chose out of the infinity of possible worlds the one that was best. This was a claim that met an often sceptical response, most famously in Voltaire's *Candide*, in which Leibniz was caricatured as Doctor Pangloss. No one but a philosopher could think that we live in the best of all possible worlds – except for a theologian: for it is hard to see why a God who was omniscient, omnipotent, and supremely good would invent a world in which there was unnecessary evil. However, even if Leibniz was orthodox in this sense he was heterodox in another. In line with the science of the day (and, largely, of ours), Leibniz's universe was a deterministic one: if God had a choice to instantiate the world that he did (and it is hard to see even there that he had much leeway, given the need to maximise goodness), once he had made that choice, it is even harder to see that there is any choice for us.

That is, once God has selected this world as the best, and instantiated it, there is no room for manoeuvre: everything in it is already chosen. In what Leibniz calls the 'complete concept' of myself is everything that I have done or will do, and this was inherent in the world from the beginning. This runs counter to our intuitions: we like to think that we could have turned left, not right, or taken another path, that our lives could have been otherwise than they are. Robert Frost famously took the road 'less travelled by, / And that has made all the difference'. Not so, for Leibniz: Frost had no option but to take the road he did. So is it for everyone. On the Leibnizian view I could not have turned left that day or taken another path, because according to the complete concept of Roger Caldwell (which can only exist in the mind of God) it was necessary to the plan of this world that I should have turned right that day and taken this path and not another. The possibility of my doing otherwise exists only as a possibility – a possibility, however, that could not have been actualised in this world but only in another of the infinity of possible worlds. In other possible worlds I *did* turn left that day: in other possible worlds are counterparts of myself who did or will do things I never did or will do in this world. It is also in other possible worlds that Don Quixote and Mrs Dalloway and Sherlock Holmes and all those others live who are fictions in this world but actualities in their own.

Philosophers, from the Greeks onwards, have often found problems in explaining how we can speak of fictional entities – as Parmenides puts it, 'For you may not know what-is-not – there is no end to it – nor may you tell of it'. To speak of something comprehensibly is in some sense to bring it into existence, if only an imaginary or conceptual one. Thus philosophers such as Meinong are sometimes led to embrace extravagant ontologies in which all sorts of entities from golden mountains to chimeras to the square root of minus one somehow bizarrely coexist in this world along with more familiar objects. Bertrand Russell hoped in his theory of descriptions to avoid such a plethora of unnecessary entities. Famously, he gave a logical analysis of the proposition, 'The present king of France is bald'. Now, this seems a meaningful proposition, is unambiguous in what it says, but it remains puzzling: in the absence of a present king of France can it be said to be true or false? For Bertrand Russell it was false, because, on his analysis, the statement claims that there is at least one thing that is the present king of France, that there is at most one thing that is the present king of France, and that that thing is bald. The statement is therefore false, because it fails to refer: in our world there is no present king of France. But, of course, its contradiction is also false: it is likewise not the case that the present king of France has a good head of hair. He is in no position to fit either option as he does not exist – at least not in *our* world.

In fiction, of course, things are different. In a fictional world – say in a novel in which the French Revolution never occurred (one that Roger Scruton might like) – there may well be a present king of France, and he may be bald, or he may have a good head of hair. Perhaps an important part of the plot may depend on the issue. But it may likewise be the case that nothing turns on the issue, so that we are not informed one way or the other, in which case the issue is undecidable: the statement that 'The present king of France is bald' has a fictional referent, but his baldness doesn't; again the statement is meaningful but is neither true nor false. Fictional worlds are not completely filled, like ours, in which every hair on our head is counted, but gappy, partial: in these worlds Hamlet is neither left- nor right-handed, Lady Macbeth has an indefinite number of children, and Mrs Dalloway might or might not like oysters. In their respective fictional worlds these are matters of no importance.

What, then, *is* of importance? If so much is indeterminate, what is essential to a fictional character, and what is accidental? We are told that Sherlock Holmes plays the violin and that he takes tobacco from a Persian slipper. Is a Sherlock Holmes who does neither still Sherlock Holmes? In fact, it seems that neither characteristic is essential – we can conceive of a Holmes who dislikes music and doesn't smoke tobacco, but not of one who failed to solve problems that others too had found insoluble, nor one who is married with three children. Such a character would simply have ceased to be Sherlock Holmes.

Similar considerations apply outside of fiction. How far can any of us have been different and yet still claim the same essential identity? T.S. Eliot, for example, might have died in his teens, might have been an absinthe-drinker, might never have written *The Waste Land*, might have worn a gold lamé suit. He would still have been T.S. Eliot for all that – if a very different one from the Eliot with whom we are familiar. But he would not have been T.S. Eliot if he had been born of different parents and in another century; there are some characteristics that are necessary if we are to still be ourselves, others that are merely possible, whether also actualised or not.

Leibniz, that universal genius, in speaking of possible worlds, was a distant progenitor of what is now known as many-worlds semantics or modal logic, dealing with the modes of necessity and possibility across and within worlds. But how are we to understand this talk of possible worlds? For Saul Kripke, 'a possible world isn't a distant country that we are coming across, or viewing through a telescope' – rather, it is a logical construct. He gives the example of a throw of two dice which results in their displaying two numbers face up. We can calculate that there are thirty-six possible states of the two dice, but only one is here instantiated, say, a three and a one. All the other thirty-five states, including the double six we hoped for, remain unsubstantiated, unfulfilled possibilities. The three and the one are instantiated in this world, what we think of as the actual world: all the remaining values belong to other possible worlds. There is our world which is not only possible but also actual; there are an infinity – or infinities – of other worlds which are possible but not actual, existing only as logical constructs, or as fictions.

In other possible worlds there exist counterparts of ourselves. We can identify them as our counterparts by reasons of our origin – being born of the same parents – but our lives and life-experiences may significantly diverge across worlds. I am currently sitting in a room, writing an essay for *PN Review*. In countless other possible worlds, other Roger Caldwells are doing the same. In one of them he gives up in despair. In another he is interrupted by a phone call, and forgets what he wanted to say. In this world, however, he goes on to complete the essay. There is a certain pathos in this: an infinity of near-identical figures doing more or less the same, and who are unaware of each other, cannot see or speak to one another, cannot ever meet. Our counterparts are the numerous possibilities we conceive for ourselves, but fail to actualise. Borges in 1934 planned in exquisite detail his own suicide, to be carried out in a room in the Hotel Delicias. As we know, he never executed the plan. In this world he lived to enjoy old age, but in another possible world the plan was executed exactly as conceived, with the result that in that world Borges killed himself in 1934.

But in speaking like this we are unwittingly falling into the trap against which Kripke warned us, of envisaging these possible worlds as somehow actual rather than merely possible, rather in the way we respond to characters in novels or dramas when we give assent to fictions. We see them as somewhere instantiated rather than as mere logical possibilities. However, according to David Lewis, in doing so we are seeing correctly. In his magisterial work *On the Plurality of Worlds* (1986), he argues eloquently for what he calls modal realism, that is, that every possibility is in some world actualised. This is the equivalent of Leibniz's God, who, having considered the infinity of possible worlds, decides on a sudden whim to actualise not just the one world, but all of them. For Lewis, God does not come into the picture (though there are presumably worlds in which God is actualised, unless he is a contradiction in terms), but he turns the tables neatly on those who would protest at this superfluity of worlds: 'What a remarkable bit of luck for us if the very world we are part of is the one that is absolutely actual! Out of all the people there are in all the worlds, the great majority are doomed to live in worlds that lack absolute actuality, but we are the select few. What reason could we ever have to think it was so?' It should be noted that these are not entirely new concerns. The Greeks, as usual, got there first. Democritus and Epicurus both calmly accepted that there was an infinity of worlds. The Stoics, by contrast, believing that the same world was endlessly repeated down to the last detail after each world-conflagration or ecpyrosis, speculated as to whether in each reconstituted world its inhabitants were identical with their predecessors or were different, thus anticipating present-day talk of counterparts.

For Lewis, when we speak of something's being actual what is meant is only that it is actual in this world – for example, that it is something we can point to. But in other worlds exactly the same situation applies. I, Roger Caldwell, actualised in this world, see my counterpart in another world as existing only in the realm of possibility. But for that Roger Caldwell in the other world, *he* is the real Roger Caldwell, and I in turn am to him only his shadowy counterpart, a possibility of existence, not actually actual, not quite real, a sort of fiction. For Lewis, then, what is seen to be actual simply depends upon what world you inhabit. Sherlock Holmes and Mrs Dalloway are fictions in this world: in others, since on Lewis's account all possibilities are somewhere actualised, Sherlock Holmes does indeed live at 221b Baker Street and Mrs Dalloway is indeed preparing for another party.

But, of course, this returns us to the extravagant ontologies that the likes of Russell and Kripke resist in the name of common sense. In these worlds exist not only Sherlock Holmes and Mrs Dalloway but all the characters in every novel or drama ever written, or that will come to be written, or that could be written, and also all conceivable creatures from talking donkeys to centaurs and basilisks. This ontological overload seems too much a mad logician's dream and the sane person's nightmare. It is even more extravagant than the solution to the paradoxes of quantum physics espoused by such multiverse theorists as David Deutsch, although Lewis deals with worlds that are complete in themselves, whereas Deutsch deals with branching worlds. In the sub-atomic world with which quantum physics is concerned what we think of as particles exist in a superimposition of states – until they are measured, or observed, in which case we have what is known as the collapse of the wave function: that is, the particle acquires a particular position or velocity. The question is: what happens to all the other values? (The issue is logically akin to Kripke's throw of the two dice, mentioned above.) Deutsch's solution is that these too are instantiated, but in worlds that branch off from this one every time there is a collapse of the wave function. Here Sherlock Holmes and Mrs Dalloway fail to make their appearance, since they were never actualised, but we ourselves do, and again, we are multiply instantiated, existing in numerous mutually inaccessible split-off worlds.

Certainly, these are dizzying prospects, but surely we have moved from fiction to science-fiction. David Lewis's book is one of the most densely argued works in modern philosophy – I have only scratched the surface of it here – but it has to be said that his brand of modal realism finds few full-blooded takers. David Deutsch's 'realist' multiverse approach to quantum physics remains a minority view among scientists – while many quantum physicists are content if the mathematics works out and simply refuse to be embroiled in ontological speculation, all the more so if it leads to such counterintuitive conclusions as those of Deutsch.

For most of us, however, we may question what difference it makes in practice whether, as with Kripke, these other possible worlds remain as logical constructs or, with Lewis (and Deutsch), they are also actualised. Is this a difference that makes no difference? After all, we cannot have access to these worlds. What my counterpart does in another world is no concern of mine – I can't reach across to him, nor he to me. There are those, however, who argue that the difference has ethical consequences. If my counterpart is merely a logical fiction it is certainly true that he is of no concern of mine. If, however, he is actualised in other worlds, he is alive in exactly the same way I am, he has had some of the same life-experiences that I have; not only this, but he exists in countless versions. At the very least this diminishes (drastically) our sense of our own uniqueness – and, potentially at least, our sense of personal responsibility. Why should I try to be good if there are already countless versions of myself that are better and countless versions that are worse? Why should I strive for perfection if elsewhere I have already achieved it, if there are countless counterparts of myself who will do the things that *I* ought to have done? The T.S. Eliot who lives in this world need not bother to write *The Waste Land* (in other worlds it is already written; in some of them it has been written by Ezra Pound); instead, knowing he was a great poet in other worlds, he might concentrate on a life of dissolution and frivolity, giving himself up to absinthe, and amassing a collection of gold lamé suits.

Needless to say, Lewis has answers to these objections, though this is not the place to adjudicate on them. I want now to move on to the obvious fact that, although in an empirical sense, we live in the one world, in another sense we inhabit numerous worlds. Sir Thomas Browne, in *Religio Medici*, famously saw man as 'that great and true Amphibium whose nature is disposed to live not onely like other creatures in divers elements, but in divided and distinguished worlds'. Unlike other animals, we see ourselves and others in terms of possibilities – of what might be, and of what might have been. We tell stories about ourselves and to ourselves about possible futures and possible pasts – some of which may be true. We inhabit pictorial, acoustic, poetic, fictional worlds, worlds made for us by artists: this is the subject-matter of Nelson Goodman's by now classic text, *Ways of Worldmaking* (1978). Of course, artists do not create *complete* worlds – but they are complete enough for their purpose. Further, what is possible in one artistic world is impossible in another – they operate according to different rules. The sound-world of Bach is distinct from that of Debussy as it is from that of Beethoven – though admittedly there are Bachian echoes in, say, the latter's Opus 110 Piano Sonata, it is nonetheless Bach transformed into Beethoven. There is a Dickensian world and a Tolstoyan one – a Pecksniff would not be at home in *War and Peace*, and it is impossible to imagine Anna Karenina in *Bleak House*. What is possible in Mallarmé's world is impossible in that of A.E. Housman: there can be no luckless lads in the former, no fauns and nymphs in the latter. We cannot live simultaneously in both Mallarmé's and Housman's worlds, but can only inhabit them successively. Further, all artistic worlds are compatible with living in *this* world. In this sense we live temporarily in innumerable different possible worlds when we flick through the pages of a poetry anthology. These worlds are not remote and inaccessible like the possible worlds of Kripke and Lewis, but ones we can inhabit: we continue to live in Emma Bovary's world even as we put the book aside and search for our ticket when arriving at Liverpool Street Station in this world.

Goodman resourcefully explores some of the ways in which artists make these new worlds. But when he goes on to note 'the very continuity and unity, the very affinity, of art and science and perception as branches of worldmaking' we must take pause. He also tells us that 'science and art proceed in much the same way with their searching and building'. But the truth is that they don't: scientists are not worldmakers in the way that artists are. Neither is there parity between living in a Newtonian or Einsteinian world on the one hand and a Tolstoyan or Dostoevskyan one on the other. Nor is it simply true, for that matter, that the Newtonian picture is false and the Einsteinian one true: simply the latter one *explains* more than the other about *this* world. Art is not progressive in this sense: Virgil does not supersede Homer, Mahler doesn't make Haydn redundant. Nor are we forced to choose between them; we can happily have both. Artists, as Nelson Goodman tells us, create new worlds – or partial worlds, or alternative sequences of this world (as Leibniz has it). But scientists don't. Their business lies entirely with this world. Instead it is the artists who create for us possible worlds – thereby immeasurably expanding the imaginative space we live in – and making it possible for us to further reflect on *this* world from the vantage-point of another.

RAYMOND QUENEAU

From Hitting the Streets

Translated by Rachel Galvin

Taxi drivers, street sweepers, a *bouquiniste,* unsuccessful prostitutes, a menaced bicycle-rider, noisy children, an old woman shunted aside in a crowd, and some disgruntled animals at the zoo populate the poems of Raymond Queneau's *Hitting the Streets.* Unreeling like a series of clips recorded during a stroll through Paris, the book is wickedly funny, but it is also a bittersweet meditation on how 'the river of forgetfulness carries away the city'. Queneau's *flâneur* is a linguist with a penchant for the odd spoken phrase as well as a photojournalist with an eye for the telling gesture of the passer-by. *Hitting the Streets,* like much of Queneau's writing, records French as it is actually spoken, or what he dubbed 'néo-français': 'C'mon missus step on it we're in a rush'.

Beloved for his smart-talking, filthy-mouthed, nine-year-old protagonist of *Zazie in the Metro,* Queneau is also known for his novel *Odile*, which skewers André Breton and other Surrealists; and a book of sonnets that has been called the longest book in the world, *One Hundred Thousand Billion Poems.* In 1960 he founded the Oulipo (Ouvroir de littérature potentielle), a group of mathematicians and writers. It still meets regularly, making it the longest-running literary group in French history.

Hitting the Streets is Queneau's love note to Paris – a Paris that is always in the process of becoming superannuated. Even as Queneau writes of contemporary issues (terrible traffic, the Vietnam War, the disappearance of public urinals) he remembers Paris of the beatnik era, World War II, and the turn of the century: 'they fill the city all the dead / it's tough not to trample them'. The volume is packed with arcane knowledge drawn from Queneau's years of writing a daily newspaper column of Paris trivia called 'Do You Know Paris?' It features odes to odd street names and a ballad to a fine cheese from Saint Maure.

But the poems also describe the tricks of perspective that can occur when trekking through the urb – such as when one rounds a corner and finds a seascape instead of a cityscape, or discovers a street that resembles a ponderous bird. *Hitting the Streets* is a paean to Paris in which Queneau catalogues 'for poposs posterity' everything from 'one Louvre museum one Place Saint-Sulpice / some chaperoned children at the flower market' to 'the banks of the Seine / one vert-galant / and some raccoons gallivanting'.

Lutèce (Lethe)

The river of forgetfulness carries away the city
with its vacation departures and New Year's Day stalls
its tourist buses its springtime lily of the valley
its July Fourteenths and its caramels
the municipal water carts of its summer its winter snows
its autumn rains that give its dust an electric odour
its shopkeepers who buy or sell their shops the changing
                                          names of bistros
the re-baptised streets the torn-down posters
the river of forgetfulness whose mythological name one
                                          even misremembers
the forgotten Lethe does not cease to flow

All Souls Generalised

This city is full of the dead
they swarm at curves in the path
    at intersection crossings
they congest the streets
they do not stop pressing by and pressing again
    deceased laundresses
they descend from roofs
climb ladders
slide through windows

they fill the city all the dead

it's tough not to trample them

in the time of hackney cabs and limos
and locals
it was anarchy
you crossed the streets as you liked
nowadays
the dead the poor dead stop at red lights
Camulogène crosses at the crosswalk
the king stands in the window of the Louvre
and Henri Beyle does not stop pacing up and down rue Neuve-
    des-Capucines

no one moves

Aerial Metro

In the shelter of the stairs
skirts fly up in the air
Passy platform close to the apple tree
of the owner of an unoccupied apartment
where, undressing,
is a lady

Rue Linné

The poor animals behind the bars of their enclosure
hear all manner of jabber
whether it's in the Jardin des Plantes or the Vincennes zoo
what balderdash they must give ear to
the poor animals behind the bars of their enclosure
deserve our pity
for having to tolerate so much hooey
but they go on grazing with composure
the poor animals in their enclosure

The Cheese from Sainte-Maure

While on my way to Auteuil
passing by rue des Belles-feuilles
I glimpsed a purple cluster
of fool choristers
trumpeting the Loire Valley
and its nutritious victuals
to melodies pure and simple
it was a real carnival
but as it was Saturday
people munched with impiety
on buttered toast and bacon
O what a pleasure to take in
the wisely fooling choristers
prattling to aficionados
about Loire Valley fodder
with regret I could not linger
but left this tasty spectacle
and continued on my way
whistling a Spanish jingle

The Concierges

For years and many a twelve-month
haven't set foot on this street
and I find once again
the old verdigrisy grey-beard
sobbing in his doorway
the concierge and her broom
the dreaming cat neither more nor less
      moth-eaten
nothing and no one has moved
only my body has crossed
 the road

The Fountains No Longer Sing

I am dying of ennui besighed the fountain
the wind subsides it will soon darken
the day wanes perhaps it will expire
perhaps it will slither by with the waters of the Seine
perhaps it will fall softly into slumber
leaving only a trail of silence
The birds are voiceless
      a shopkeeper closes the shutters
  of his shop
     someone walks by with freshly bought
         bread
I am dying of ennui besighed the fountain

Rue Paul Verlaine

Sometimes I have a strange, penetrating vision
of a street made of off-white and maternal tin
on either side the walkway beats like a wing
while the road bears all the weight of its being.

Into the pond, the pure lead sewers drip
engulfing a mouth at an immortal gape
hopscotch games are etched at either tip
which the average applicant does not navigate

Below a titanium sky a lone roof on a wander
slowly begins to travel above the structures
where a creature prowls with my sister's features

Calm with its hazy, imitation sicamour
This road has the sulky amaranth glamour
of coming to a close without losing its odour.

Elsewhere

A street like any other
in an indeterminate arrondissement
maybe in the sixteenth
suddenly
right when you least expected it
you see at the bottom of the cliff
a port
at the shore
of the sea
you may waver between Le Havre and Yport
the waves sleep
ships immobile but absent
figure in this milky landscape
you'd think it a tourist spot
lightly sanded down
then you continue on your way
and you arrive by rue Férou
at Place Saint-Sulpice

Raymond Queneau: from Hitting the Streets

The Translatory Tower

The Eiffel Tower is losing its hair
this is a spinster's filamentary issue
Christ is also the filial issue of a spinster
go translate that into French for me!

The Paris of Paroles
(inventory)

One Eiffel tower one Caucasian tomb
one Place Pigalle one Jardin des Plantes
one arc de triomphe one Seine one Place de la Concorde
one bird market one for flowers another for scrap metal
two hundred and twenty-two rues de Vaugirard
thirty-three rues de Ménilmontant
one grand palais one Gare Saint-Lazare
one street of the last of the Mohicans
one rue de Tolbiac one canal de l'Ourcq
the two Tuileries ponds
one rue de Seine
   and another Vaugirard

one caserne de la pépinière two rues de Rome
   and another Gare Saint-Lazare

one rue de Rennes one rue de l'Échaudé
one Luxemburg one Porte Champerret
   and another grand palais
one Montsouris park one avenue des Gobelins
one rue de Bercy one cours des halles
one Louvre museum one Place Saint-Sulpice
some chaperoned children at the flower market
an aerial metro a large boulder
   and some more halles

some innocents some blancs-manteaux
a few rosiers one king of Sicily
one maternity ward one salpetrière
one carousel one gas company
   the banks of the Seine
one vert-galant
        and some raccoons gallivanting

The Flies

The flies of today
are no longer the flies of yore
they are less cheerful
heavier, more majestic, more serious
more conscious of their scarcity
they know the threat of genocide
In my childhood they joyfully went on gluing themselves
to paper meant to kill them
by the hundreds, maybe the thousands
they went on shutting themselves
in specially shaped bottles
by the hundreds, maybe the thousands
they skated, skulked, and perished
by the hundreds, maybe the thousands
they abounded
they were really living
Now they watch their step

the flies of today
are no longer the flies of yore

The Flies Again

It happened back a number of years
that I traheaved
the cartage of my souvenirs
to a time when I believed
that a hillock in solitude
awaited its explorer
and that I was that dummy
I drove myself on intrepidly
up at the hillock's summit
as soon as I reached my target
with its delicious clamour
of lovely flies and their fragrance
rustling like birds and laying,
those creatures of virulence,
the eggs of maggots forthcoming
the hill was full to capacity
and I contemplated the fervour
then the muscids took flight
bearing with them their whole burden
and I stayed upon this site
to traheave once again

Paris Deacon

At the end of rue Mouffetard
in front of church Saint-Médard
a little old man waits for a little old woman
the little old woman was at confession
she arrives all pleased
that didn't last, says she, more than five minutes
the little old man makes no comment
stumbling along they set off again
in the direction of the Vatican

ROBERT GRIFFITHS

Shelley and the Old and New Atheism

Two hundred years ago, Shelley was expelled from Oxford University for atheism. More precisely, he was expelled for not admitting, and not denying, at a hearing called by the Master and Fellows of University College, that he was in fact the author of the pamphlet *The Necessity of Atheism*. He was effectively expelled for insubordinate silence. His apparent shock at this sits innocently with the effort he had made to ensure discomfort to others, having sent copies of his work to all the bishops, and to the heads of all the university colleges. Unlike the more urbane non-theist, David Hume, whose spirit moves closely over the surface of Shelley's brief work, the poet was not prepared, or not disingenuous enough, to post intellectual arguments for atheism and then diplomatically deny that he actually held such views himself. Hume had said, famously, that he did not believe in the existence of atheists.

Yet, as a stepping stone across the river of disbelief, *The Necessity of Atheism* is a small and slippery place to stand. While it has been called the first printed avowal of atheism in England, it is not clear that we can even give it Richard Holmes' faint praise, 'neat and effective'.[1] It is highly derivative, largely repeating in less forceful ways the arguments of Hume's *Dialogues concerning Natural Religion* and those of the influential French *philosophe*, the Baron d'Holbach, author of the much more substantial attack on God, *Système de la Nature*. More worryingly, perhaps, in its rather prudish use of philosophical jargon and its high-mindedness, it lacks the sincerity, as well as the deft sardonicism, of the work of earlier and more passionate atheists, such as the priest Jean Meslier, who left his apostasy to be read, and appreciated by Voltaire, after his death. Still, Shelley was but 18.

Today, of course, we have New Atheism, and apparently a new atheism debate. At the centre of New Atheism is the biologist Richard Dawkins, author of *The God Delusion*, over which Hume's spirit moves almost as closely as over Shelley's work. Close to the centre is a modern d'Holbach, the materialist philosopher Daniel Dennett, author of *Breaking the Spell*, an attempt to provide a reductive, evolutionary account of the source of religious belief. Then loosely associated with these are the neuroscientist Sam Harris and more diverse authors such as Christopher Hitchens. Reading this material, it is noticeable how the New Atheism debate goes over a great deal of ground that had been very hard worked in the older atheism debate that broke out in the late eighteenth century and which provided the intellectual backdrop to Shelley's early development. In this prior debate, Hume, d'Alembert, Helvétius, Diderot, d'Holbach, Voltaire and others provided a sustained assault on theism that is not matched by contemporary writing. Against these 'infidels', in Britain at least, Joseph Priestley was to write reams in a heroic attempt to reconcile Christianity, philosophy and natural science.[2] In the current debate, the role of Priestley seems to have fallen to the indefatigable Alister McGrath, author of *Dawkin's God* and *The Dawkins Delusion*.

Of course, these two debates do have differences. New Atheism is largely driven by evolutionary thinking. But it is clear that neither Hume's arguments nor those of d'Holbach (or Shelley) *require* the truth of evolution. All these writers thought that philosophy and science had *already* made belief in the existence of God untenable. D'Holbach argued, bluntly, that 'Man ... is the work of nature ... He exists in Nature ... He is submitted to the laws of Nature ... He cannot deliver himself from them',[3] in short that the universe, and man, are *purely* natural things governed by natural law. A Victorian public that had been familiar with such a position for up to a hundred years might not have flinched as much as it did from the implications of Darwin's. There is another interesting difference. In the late eighteenth century, the atheism debate arose from the intellectual foment that led up to and beyond the French Revolution. In Britain, this made it relatively easy to view atheism as a belief system, or lack-of-belief system, that merely led to violence and anarchy. This was one of the reasons why, in Britain, public expression of atheism, such as Shelley's, was problematic. Today, by contrast, the New Atheism debate is spurred by the alleged developing tensions between Christian and Islamic cultures. Sam Harris is concerned that both Islamic fundamentalism and the Christian fundamentalism that seems to influence thinking in the United States are leading to social unrest, terrorism and war. Nowadays, atheism is partly seen as an antidote to religious extremism, whereas in late-eighteenth-century Britain, atheism itself – Shelley included – was seen as a threat to the stability of Christian society.

What is striking about Shelley's contribution to the atheism debate is, of course, the fact that he is a poet and not, primarily, a philosopher or natural scientist. There is, actually, something slightly uncomfortable in watching the young Shelley put on his philosopher's cloak, or scientist's lab coat, in order to storm the churches. He awkwardly decants some interesting assumptions for a poet. We are told, 'A close examination of the validity of the proofs adduced to support any proposition is the only secure way of attaining truth'.[4] Later we are given, 'no testimony can be admitted which is contrary to reason; reason is founded on the evidence of the senses'. What is slightly odd is that any *poet* should believe such things, that only reason conceived narrowly, or the evidence of the senses, provide us with secure ways of attaining truth.

What is then clear is that either as he wrote, or pretty soon after, even Shelley did not *really* believe these things, as it became obvious to him that poetry was a different kind of discovery process to philosophy and science; that the poet was able to *show* truth in symbol and image, and that the truths shown in this way were not necessarily open to rational demonstration, nor did they necessarily stand in any clear-cut relationship to the evidence of the senses. In the Preface to *Alastor*, written in 1815, he had moved beyond the narrowly rational empiricism of *The Necessity of Atheism* to talk of how the poet unites the 'intellectual faculties, the imagination, the functions of sense ... attaching them to a single image'. Then in the Preface to *The Revolt of Islam*, written a couple of years later, he recognises how poetry is capable of a persuasive force quite different to that of rational or evidential demonstration. Conceding that he has made no attempt to advocate the political 'messages' of his poem, 'by methodical and systematic argument', he says he has chosen rather to 'only awaken the feelings, so that the reader should see the beauty of true virtue'. In this last phrase he appears to concede that it is possible, in poetry, to communicate truth *entirely* through the awakening of feeling.

Had he applied insights of this kind to his discussion of religious belief, one imagines that the results would have been very different to *The Necessity of Atheism*. It is possible that he would have recognised that, for many, belief in God has nothing to do with what can be rationally demonstrated or supported by sense experience, that God is, as Karen Armstrong puts it in her marvellous *History of God*, 'a product of the creative imagination',[5] and that the worship of God is this creative imagination in practice. Still, it is possible that Shelley, like many atheists, and like all of the New Atheists, would not have been content with this, and would have still felt the need to apply philosophical and scientific method to the *disproof* of God's existence.

Shelley would probably be disappointed at where we are now – even given his later intellectual and imaginative development: to see that views he thought he had comprehensively dispatched, further to their comprehensive dispatch by prior thinkers, were still in the unresolved process of being dispatched by later writers, using much the same arguments, and that there remained at least one neo-Priestley standing solidly for them, using much the same arguments. But it might well be asked whether the heat and sound of the debate surrounding New Atheism would be half so warm or loud if those contributing to it and reading through it were more familiar with the territory that had already been explored in the older one. On reflection, one presumes that this particular kind of atheist debate is *bound* to recur, sooner or later, because we are *bound* to have forgotten, or never read, the works of those dead two hundred years who held pretty much the same views – for or against – as some of us do today. In the year 2211, one can be sure that someone will submit a piece to *PNR*, lamenting the fact that those then debating the pros and cons of religious belief will have forgotten, or never read, their Dawkins and their McGrath. They may even ask us to remember poor Shelley.

Notes
1   Richard Holmes, *Shelley: The Pursuit* (New York: Harper, 2003), Ch. 2.
2   See Martin Priestman, *Romantic Atheism, Poetry and Freethought 1780–1830* (Cambridge: Cambridge University Press, 1999), Ch. 1.
3   Baron d'Holbach, *Système de la Nature, Vol 1, Part 1, Chapter 1*, Freethought Archives Kindle Edition (1770, tr. 1820).
4   P.B. Shelley, *The Necessity of Atheism and Other Essays* (New York: Prometheus Books, 1993), p. 30.
5   Karen Armstrong, *A History of God* (London: Vintage, 2011).

Build and maintain your own website with ease - from under £9 a month.

With the growth of the internet, writers now want their own websites to preview their latest publications, communicate with their readers, and present themselves to the world. Without technical expertise, this can be a daunting task, and professional help can be hugely expensive.

WebGuild is your solution for both new and replacement websites.

WebGuild can be used on *any* computer with internet access. No other software is required. Password protection means that you can maintain your site safely and securely from anywhere in the world, and with email addresses included in the package you can be in constant contact. Professional design completes your route to the perfect website.
    We also provide support to help you get your site up and running.

Authors already using **WebGuild** include David Kinloch, John Gallas, Sebastian Barker, Grevel Lindop, James Sutherland-Smith, and Andrew Waterman. Visit www.webguild.co.uk for links to their sites and more information about all of our services.

E-mail: enquiries@webguild.co.uk
Or write to: WebGuild Media Ltd
                    47 Church Road, Gatley, Cheshire. SK8 4NG.
Telephone: 0161 428 1102
Website: www.webguild.co.uk

Learning how to use the software is surprisingly quick and, once mastered, uploading data is as easy as falling out of bed
- John Harper
(www.johnharperpublishing.co.uk)

The package is easy to set up, even for idiots like me; good on the eye; and simple to maintain.
- Chris McCully
(www.chrismccully.co.uk)

I'm continually amazed at hearing how much other writers are paying for their sites, and how little they get for their money. My site has already generated enough extra work to pay for itself several times over.
- Grevel Lindop
(www.grevel.co.uk)

WebGuild

Special Offer for PN Review readers — Mention *PN Review* when ordering and receive a 10% discount on your first year's costs, including design and building

HESTER KNIBBE

Five Poems

Translated by Jacquelyn Pope

After the Flood

After the Flood there you sit
next to the boat, the fish
gasping for air, the hare finding
nothing to eat yet and all the birds

left behind. There you sit
in the same skirt in which, waters ago,
you boarded the ship, but the dance
has drained from your feet. For once the rain

blew over at last, the water
was lulled mirror-smooth, you saw

your world turned upside down and lower still
any movement stalled for good and
when you took a better look that too
that image stayed with you and how

with each glance your essence
lost more depth. Now you sit,
ram and ewe already on dry ground,
all at sea in flotsam and jetsam.

Standing

Turned to stone I stand on this earth
in a long skirt and a shawl
that he pinned close across my breasts
because the world insists
on it. That's how I was raised.

My eyes have neither iris nor pupil
so I look to the inside, want to hear
there everything that happens outside.

From what I observe a smile
lies frozen around my lips
that just keeps freezing. Thaw me
adorn me with a cap of blooms
and long stalks in my body.

Psalm 4631

In my need I call out
to nothing and to no one, I am silent. One who's
seen dust gone to dust and bygones and survives

has forgotten how to cry. Let the oak moan
and groan about leaves fallen
too early to the ground, the branch

torn off its trunk. Let me stand wordless
in its shadow. Let

my silence be not small and stooped
but worthily high
and broad as the crown of the tree

now its roots and silence
are fastened to him and prayer
is smothered in the ground

Homecoming

I dreamed that I dreamed
of you: we sat on the sofa
and talked a while, you wore the sweater I'd
worn that day, your hair was
wet from all the rain. Your body, solid

and warm, was once again as fresh
as when you'd been down in the fen
and you recounted animatedly
how different beyond turned out to be,
how deep the roots
of the oak went down. And I

told you what I'd experienced
up here, how the hazel
had grown. And what a year
for spiders, I said. You burst out laughing.

Handling

Dead ordinary it seemed that night,
sitting with strangers at a wooden table
worn smooth with use, somewhere
in a house on a grass steppe. Those people

stared so at us when
the plates and dishes appeared
on the table that I thought: that's it,
the food is poisoned, they know
all about it. And I also thought: oh,

I'll just eat it anyway. Then we were
herded outside in silence, to the zinc
gutter low along the wall and there
they hacked off both our hands.
We stood there, bleeding to death.

MARIUS KOCIEJOWSKI

Once Upon a Time in County Cork

One Woman's Journey from there to an Area of Manifest Greyness

The Irish poet and novelist Martina Evans (née Cotter) when it came time came for her to paint her living room she sought to replicate the blue of the covers of the Shakespeare & Company first edition of *Ulysses* (1922). James Joyce permeates, no, *soaks*, her talk. 'Chrysostom is mentioned on the very first page,' she told me with all the zeal of one who has just opened up a pharaoh's tomb. 'What Joyce is actually referring to are the gold fillings and the well-fed mouth of Malachi Mulligan. A bit later, in the Proteus episode, he compares his own teeth to empty shells and calls himself "toothless Kinch, the superman". Joyce had terrible problems with his teeth. When he went to Paris he screamed with every mouthful of French onion soup.' She paused. 'What do you call it? *Onion* soup? You don't call it *French* onion soup when you are in France, do you?'

When she speaks – softly, quickly, cramming more words into a minute than many people do in five – even the asides have asides. And there's the lovely turn of phrase too. She mentioned some woman having eloped with a sewing machine. What can it mean, I ask myself. What does it matter, though? There is a zone where all such verbal felicities are poetically rather than literally comprehensible. It set me to wondering whether in this world journey through London the most unfathomable of all countries is not the one from whence my subject comes.

'Anyway,' she continued, 'when he was drinking *that well-known Paris delight* he would scream in agony because his teeth were in such a bad state. Dental envy lies behind the whole first chapter of *Ulysses* and people don't see that! They make all these references to "Golden Mouth" but –'

'Surely,' I interjected, 'the epithet relates to Chrysostom's gift for oratory.'

'It is about that too, but what Joyce is *really* saying is that Mulligan is well fed, properly looked after. There are so many references to poverty in *Ulysses* and in particular that of the Dedalus family. Bloom is conscious of that too, when he looks at the ragged children in the street. Buck Mulligan talks about it in the very first episode when the old woman comes in with the milk, saying that if everyone could have good milk like that the country wouldn't be full of rotten teeth. Money and teeth – they're very connected.'

Odontology may form the greater part of Martina's psychological profile. She thinks teeth, she talks teeth. She writes about teeth. *Can Dentists Be Trusted?* is the title of one of her poetry collections and staring from its cover is a terrifying-looking nurse with Richard E. Grant eyes. The poem 'Gas' speaks of how 'cold thin air / breathed through a mask / changed the din of the drill / into the pure art / of Jimi Hendrix's guitar'. Another poem about dentists describes 'the ones you only visit once'. She even dreams about them. She relates a dream in which there is an IRA-like funeral for one of her extracted teeth, a tricolour over its minuscule coffin, balaclava'd men firing a salute over it. The subconscious, she tells me, is a funny place.

She loves westerns. Cowboys adorn her bathroom, a whole posse of them above the sink – the images or, rather, the *idea* of them, always preferable, she admits, to the grizzled reality from whence they come. She not so long ago watched *Rio Grande* because she had heard that at some point in the film a UFO appears in the sky behind the actors' heads. ('I was looking out for it but was so blown away by the chemistry between Maureen O'Hara and John Wayne I missed the UFO episode.') She kept rewinding the video but each time, swept up by the romance, she missed it. The Old West took her back to James Joyce. She had been watching the commentary on the filming of *The Wild Bunch* when one of its makers said that all the while he was reading the *Iliad*. Thus spurred, Martina read it and, after that, the *Odyssey* which in turn, after a hiatus of twenty years, led her back to *Ulysses*.

The cats rule, though. Donny, Dora and Alice are bigger than James Joyce, bigger than John Wayne. A conversation with her is, by extension, a conversation with them. The garden behind is, or will later be, their cemetery. Martina gave me pinkish brandy made from the elderberries that grow above one of their graves. We drank the blood of Eileen Murphy, who one day confabulated with her, or at least did so in one of Martina's most celebrated poems, 'The Day My Cat Spoke to Me'.

> I was surprised not so much by the fact
> that she spoke
> but by the high opinion she had of me.
> 'I think you're great,' she said
> and it was at this point
> I looked at her in surprise.
> 'I mean,' she continued, 'the way
> you've managed to write anything at all!'

Eileen Murphy, 'her yellow eyes opening wide / before narrowing into benevolent slits', addressed Martina at a major juncture in her life, her divorce.

'It's a dark place to go,' she said, 'I appeared in court sixteen times.'

She pointed to the crucifix she was wearing, its purpose, I suspect, more apotropaic than religious. It was a posthumous Christmas present from Eileen Murphy, the purchase of which was aided and abetted by Martina's daughter, Liadáin. Christmas saw Eileen Murphy in the grave. Martina took up wearing crosses because, she says, she has always had a problem with boundaries.

'This is my church, the Church of Eileen Murphy. It would be a kind of *Boy's Own* way of learning to live your life. If you are in a situation you would ask, "What would Eileen Murphy do?" She might hit you with a belt or a stony silence, one or the other, or maybe just a miaow. Those are probably the only responses you need in life. She is an alter ego for me. I really would like to have her kind of character, one that doesn't stand for any nonsense. I am always getting involved in nonsense.'

The walls are not quite the right shade of blue, at least not to my eye, but maybe the more she penetrates the heart and soul of her Book of Books the closer she'll come, with the next coat, or maybe the one after that, to achieving that special Greek flag blue. She was quietly amazed when I told her that in 1984 I handled the diagonally striped blue-and-white tie that Joyce wore, which he presented to the printers of *Ulysses* as the blue of his choice. The tie he later gave to his close associate, the Jewish-Russian émigré, Paul Léon, and decades later, after its stopover at the London antiquarian booksellers for whom I used to work, it is in Tulsa, Oklahoma, along with such treasures as the corrected proofs of *Finnegans Wake* and a white porcelain lion, a punning gift which Joyce gave Léon, who only a few years later perished in one of the Nazi death camps.

A chunk of Irish landscape crackled in the fireplace, one of the *Bord na Móna* (The Board of Turf) peat briquettes that Martina buys here in London. When I looked out the window onto Balls Pond Road, what Peter Ackroyd in his *London, A Biography* describes as 'an area of manifest greyness and misery', a phrase which Martina adopted for the title of one of her poems, I wondered at how in a very few lines she manages to set the tranquillity of inside against the noise of what goes on outside.

> I sleep high on the bird's nest.
> Trucks and lorries shake the house
> and make the bricks tremble,
> roaring tidal waves rock the bed
> and put me to sleep.
> There are odd wrecked Georgian houses
> beached between tyre shops and takeaways.
> Sometimes people are murdered.
> Police sirens shriek up and down all day
> like seagulls chasing sandwiches.

Disquietude is never far away, just an ably thrown pebble's click against the boarded-up front of what used to be the Turkish community library directly opposite, TOPLUM KÜTÜPHANESI, where not so long ago a young man working there hanged himself. Martina spoke of the ambulances, the police, the young Turkish men in black walking up and down the street, sorrowing for one of their tribe. Meanwhile, in her poem, 'the uniformed Catholic children / slip along the wet pavement / like blue fish / swimming down the Balls Pond Road'.

§

She comes from a village not far from Mallow in County Cork. One might be forgiven for thinking Burnfort is a mythical place. So small it has escaped the cartographer's eye, it takes its name from an ancient ringfort known as *Ráth an Tóiteáin* ('Fort of the Burnings'), of which all that remains is a souterrain – unless, of course, one wishes to include the shield on the BP sign that swung throughout the whole of her youth beside the Cotter residence, which was home, shop, bar and petrol pump all rolled into one. The family lived upstairs, a child's fantasy of a place, which in the 1940s had been owned by a scrap merchant who added all sorts of curious features – a fireplace edged with black-and-white tiles of Grecian figures, wooden panelling from a luxury liner that had been wrecked off the coast of Cork, with the cabin numbers **118, 117, 116** still visible, in black against ivory plates, a section of railway track holding up the kitchen ceiling and other oddities. And with it being Burnfort's social and mercantile centre it is also the setting, although nowhere does it say so, of Martina's as yet unpublished book, *Petrol, a Poem in Three Acts*.

A couple of things make this image special: the extensive creases and the long shadows of those who are no longer about to throw them. One of the major strands in Martina's work is that by making them talk, talk and talk she brings those shadows back to life.

'There is a lot of sound in it,' she said of her new work. 'The BP sign, the big one in the picture, swings all the time. What made me think of it is the opening scene of the movie *Once Upon a Time in the West* where all the different noises make their own music. The cowboy setting, the Deep South, the music and everything, can be related in so many ways to Ireland, to Burnfort in particular. It's about voice too. Voice is everything for me. It was Joyce's favourite instrument. I'm nothing like him, of course – I'm so simple and he's so complicated – but my first novel *Midnight Feast* is very much about voice. There are true incidents in *Petrol*. A magician came to the school once. I was grown up to the size

Marius Kociejowski: Once Upon a Time in County Cork

I am now, maybe thinner ... I grew to my full height when I was thirteen and went around for years thinking I was a giant. The magician had a big fluffy white rope and said he would hang me upside down from the ceiling where everyone could see my figure. These images come back to me, especially that awful feeling when you are young and vulnerable and everyone is about to look at you and how terrible it is going to be. The book is about how adults can confuse and terrify children. I was terrified for months after this experience. I wasn't sure if this man wouldn't come after me with his rope and force me to hang upside down. After all, he was supposed to be a magician.'

'What about your parents?'

'They went to Australia with five children, came back with seven and left two behind. They paid full price to go there, while everyone else went there for a tenner. They didn't know about the Australians offering Irish immigrants almost free passage. It was an expensive cruise. My mother told me that all the while they were on the ship they entertained people. All the children would get up and sing for them. They were in Australia for ten years. My father got sick there. They never talked much about what they did there but it was difficult for my mother, possibly difficult for my father too although he made it sound romantic when he came back. There were all these lovely aboriginal names and of course he spoke about the birds and the wildlife. He was always imitating the laugh of the kookaburra.

> My father's lips pursed with pleasure
> when he uttered the name of a place called Geelong,
> as if he was getting ready to blow
> into an invisible didgeridoo.
>   (from 'The Australian Rug')

'They lost money hand over fist and barely got back to Ireland with enough to make a fresh start. They went to County Cork. They were originally from County Limerick where they had a big farm. The farmhouse was supposed to be haunted. My poem "Stones" is about how the stories about it haunted me:

> the horse that went mad from a brain haemorrhage
> circling and circling around the hawthorn-ringed field,
> the riding accidents, bodies on the railway tracks,
> Johnny the dead dog the children buried up to its neck.

'They sold it to a man and six months later he was thrown from a horse and killed. My brother spoke of footsteps on the stairs. Maybe it was difficult for them on that lonely farm but they had it hard in Australia too. My father was struck down by rheumatic fever for most of a year and then he was knocked over by a drunken driver. He was 58 and my mother about 40 when they returned to Cork, which was when I came along, the *mistake*. They didn't know anything about running a business but they opened up the bar, shop and petrol pump. It was the focus of everything. People would come down from church, funerals, weddings, the hunt, the creamery, and it was run very haphazardly. Can you imagine, starting all over again at that age? And then a tenth child arriving just when they must have thought they had enough?'

'What about your childhood?'

'Dreamy. I had a world of my own but then I'd talk my head off if I got a chance. I had a lot of friendships with older men, which I suppose is bound to happen when you grow up in a pub – lovely old men like Tom Twomey who would play cards with me, and there was Gerald Regan, a solicitor who would bring me beautiful children's books. Rilke says the source of all poetry is childhood and dreams. We drink from the well until we drink it dry. I think that is really true. There's an interesting Graham Greene essay about how the books we read in childhood are books of divination. I believe some of the things that make us sad when we are young do so precisely because we know they are going to happen to us. And then Declan Kiberd has written about how Joyce fell in love with the story of Ulysses when he was twelve – it was the children's version by Charles Lamb that originally captured his imagination.'

In her poem 'Facing the Public' the daughter captures the mother whole, or could it be, rather, that with so much of the poem hijacked by her voice, the mother captures the daughter whole?

> My mother never asked like a normal person, it was
> *I'm asking you for the last time, I'm imploring you
> not to go up that road again late for Mass.*
>
> She never had slight trouble sleeping, it was
> *Never, never, never for one moment did I get a wink,
> as long as my head lay upon that pillow.*
>
> She never grumbled, because *No one likes a grumbler,
> I never grumble but the pain I have in my two knees this*
>   *night*
> *there isn't a person alive who would stand for it.*
>
> ...
>
> She didn't do the Stations of the Cross
> she sorrowed the length and breadth of the church.
> And yet, she could chalk up a picture in a handful of
>   words
>
> conjure a person in a mouthful of speech ...

There is very little in Martina's poetry that does not come from either her or her mother's memories. The poem becomes a study in embarrassment. It is about the mother acting out scenarios in private and then being embarrassed when she is overheard. Anyone who comes from a small place will know how there the echoes go on forever.

> Never, never, never would she be able, as long as she
>   lived,
> even if she got Ireland free in the morning, no, no, no
> she would never be able to face the public again.

'That poem came when one day my daughter Liadáin was going on about something or other and I said to her, "Don't be so dramatic". She said, "Oh, *I'm* dramatic, am I!" She made me laugh and then I thought of my mother. And the poem just came out. The strong ones tend to, but really I'd been writing it for years. She was a larger than life character, a woman who ran everything. When I told her my first book was accepted she said, "Oh, a book!" When I added that it was poetry, she replied, "Oh, poems ... I thought it was a *book*." And then she'd say things like, "As Peggy Looney said to me, 'What a book you'd write, Mrs Cotter, the interesting life you've led, if you only had the time.'" Now I feel she is writing mine. Her voice is present in so many of the poems, especially the recent ones. She will always be renewing herself through them, I suppose. A strong light casts a strong shadow. She was fantastic in a way but terrible as well. You could ring her up and put the phone down, go off, water the garden, go to Sainsbury's, come back, sweep the house, and she would *still* be talking. She wouldn't have drawn breath and if you did try to interrupt her, you'd get from her, "Will you let me *speak*!" My mother always felt she had to jump into a conversation with *something*. She had to fill in the spaces, juggle with words, and entertain people. Eileen Murphy doesn't feel that pressure, does she? She doesn't need to say the "right" thing. She just stares at you.'

§

The burnings of historical memory, 'the fort of the burnings', might be said to have been later ghosted in the domestic activities of Martina's father, who loved to set fires.

He was a quiet man,
a secret man, who liked to be alone,
and he had ten children.

He couldn't bear to cut down his trees

Every Christmas he defiantly brought in
the worst pine, with the scantiest branches,
and his family spent the whole Christmas
trying to cover it up.

Passionate about fires, inside or out,
he spent summer evenings tending crowds
of them in a field full of sunset.

(from 'A Quiet Man')

'There's something very pagan in those lines,' I said.

'He was a *real* pagan! He loved fires. There is another short poem, "Burning Rubbish", in which I describe him as standing still among the blazes like a Roman general. Before he died it seemed some mad dream to be a writer but his death was the catalyst. Daddy died when I was 27 and I was devastated. I didn't expect it ... he was an old man with cancer ... his time had come. I dreamt that I was stitching his dead body up, trying to make it come back to life like with Pangloss in *Candide*, which I was studying at the time, but he just smiled and shook his head as if he was very tired. I was so upset and in all my madness and ranting, the self-consciousness melted away. Life was too short for that and so I started writing poems. The original impulse was to write a poem about him. I couldn't do it. I had made many attempts but they all fell flat. It wasn't until I was close to completing my fourth book that I was in Waitrose one day and wrote "A Quiet Man" in two minutes on the back of my shopping list. It came out just like that. It must have been growing inside me. You could say that poem took two minutes to write or it took nine years. He was quite a bit older than my mother, a background man, not a big talker, although until he was seventy he worked really hard at some job or other as well as tearing round, looking after the garden and all the animals. A really lovely, cherubic-looking man with beautiful skin, all smiles, he'd walk our dog Fifi to the church. People would say of him, "Mr Cotter is always the gentleman, no airs or graces about him, every day going with his little dog to the church." Fifi loved the church, especially at Christmas time with the crib and the straw. The Three Wise Men arriving on January 6th always made him bark. He seemed to think they were a sinister addition. Most of all he loved to roll on the strip of orange carpet before the altar. I went up with them once. Fifi lifted his leg and Daddy just stood there, beaming with pride as Fifi pissed on the carpet. He told me it was "only a small bit", shook his head as if to say, why would anyone mind. Anything Fifi enjoyed was fantastic and sacred and probably a tribute to the orange carpet. The way my father was, well, he was a bit tangential or whatever, not exactly your normal or conventional character. All this stuff with the cats and the dogs, they were more real to him than people. My mother used to say, "There's more thought of cats and dogs than Christians in this house." Probably the same could be said for *this* house. In some ways my father never grew up. He did not want to go to school, resisted it violently. I heard the story that he rolled in the mud of the schoolyard in his new suit and eventually his mother just kept him at home. He lived in a world of his own, which made it difficult for my mother who was always branded as the bad one, but although she was tough and hard at times *somebody* had to rule, I suppose. She was super-sensitive as well ... we all were. It made for lots of dramatics and my father would have his hand on the handle of the back door, always looking to escape our racket.'

'The three-card trick men used to come to the horse fairs. My father must have remembered them from when he was little. There was a famous horse fair in Cahirmee and the three-card trick men would go there, rangy-looking fellows in flat caps who'd go to all the fairs and carnivals. You would have to *find the lady*, guess which card was where. They would first come to the pub in Burnfort and ask my father for a cardboard box, which they'd set up for their cards and my father would go weak with excitement. A man in his seventies, he'd cry, "They're here, the three-card men! They're here!"'

'Were they tinkers?'

'They were what my mother would describe as "next door to tinkers". I don't know if they were tinkers. She told me a story once about a real tinker and Tom Twomey and Lord Harrington and how they all sat by the fire, discussing horses. And because it was about horses the class differences completely melted away. That story always struck me. That's what's so important about being a poet, the *passion*. You see the most awful people, once they begin to speak of such things they are completely transformed.'

It seems as good a way as any to describe Martina's poetry, as a process of transformation which comes though allowing people their say, where even the Paddy Caseys of this world are given a shot at redemption, their awfulness made sublime. It is also a poetic world in which people tug hard at their leashes.

'My mother was much more in thrall to those particularly Irish Catholic inhibitions than my father was. I used to think it was just his personality and also the fact that women tended to be the more religious ones when I was growing up, but somebody told me that the Catholic church had been more relaxed, more Italian, before De Valera came to power and, with the help of his henchman, Archbishop McQuaid, ruled Ireland in that particularly moralistic way. My father grew up before that time, whereas my mother would have had the full weight of their influence. It was so repressed. Also De Valera was born out of wedlock, sent home from America by his mother to be brought up by his grandmother in Limerick. My poem "Reprisal" begins, "Never trust a Palatine or a Bastard." They used to say that in County Limerick "the Bastard" referred to De Valera. His mother went on to have a legitimate family in America but she never sent for him. That could be the root of his conservatism and control freakery – a personal interest in keeping women at home by the fire. You could say the political came from the personal.'

Martina pulled a 1950s Australian bible from the shelf and thumped it down in front of me. The dust rose from it and landed mote by mote in my glass of wine. I opened it onto a garish colour plate captioned 'Queen Assumed into Heaven', the Virgin Mary as I had never seen her before, a Tallulah Bankhead figure, the synthetic blue of her robe clashing with the synthetic pink of her dress, not colours such as one might find in nature – although maybe that was the point, that those chemically induced hues only served to emphasise the supernatural. Maybe, though, they were merely the colours of a tacky decade.

'Oh yes, I think that is so very Disney. It reminds me of *Sleeping Beauty* when at the end of the film she twirls round and round, her dress going pink and blue, pink and blue. You will notice a lot of pink and blue in the house. The thing about religion is the iconography. Ever since I was a child I've loved the colours, the colours of suffering, the Virgin Mary blue, the pinks and blues. Our family bible has exactly the colours I like. There is a whole generation very nostalgic about the iconography, especially those of us who have left the Church. We spent ages looking at this stuff. We had no choice. We should have come to hate it but because we got away, looking back on it now we can love it. Everything seems to come full circle.'

'So God's still kicking about your psyche?'

'I would never be so foolish as to think I could ever escape Him,' she whispered. 'There is a poem of mine "One Morning in July" which laughs at my younger self thinking I could strike out as an atheist. But I think I've left the Church. Ireland is in a very bad state with it, it's reeling at the moment. I heard the bishop isn't coming to the latest confirmation in a particular parish. Somebody said he'd be afraid to come because he'd be lynched. This is because of all the recent scandals, the bishops covering up for paedophiles. The feeling is *that* bad. Originally Ireland was a matriarchy with very strong female figures. Brigid was a goddess before she became a saint and it can't have been good when these powerful, pagan, rounded, female figures had to be squeezed into a virgin mould. All the stories about St Patrick and St Brigid are very interesting, with his being all about sexual repression and suffering and hers about abundance. When the goddess Brigid passed cows they would give three times the milk. She was like a corn goddess. She could hang her coat on a sunbeam. She was very much associated with the sun, with fertility, with abundance, with snakes, with giving milk … and then St Patrick arrived. One of the stories that really sums him up relates how one of the chieftains decided to convert to Christianity and St Patrick had this crosier which he went to stick into the earth but it went through the chieftain's foot by mistake and the chieftain, thinking this was part of the Christian initiation rites, did not utter a word throughout the whole thing. *That* set the tone for the way we were going to be from then on. I have no time for St Patrick.'

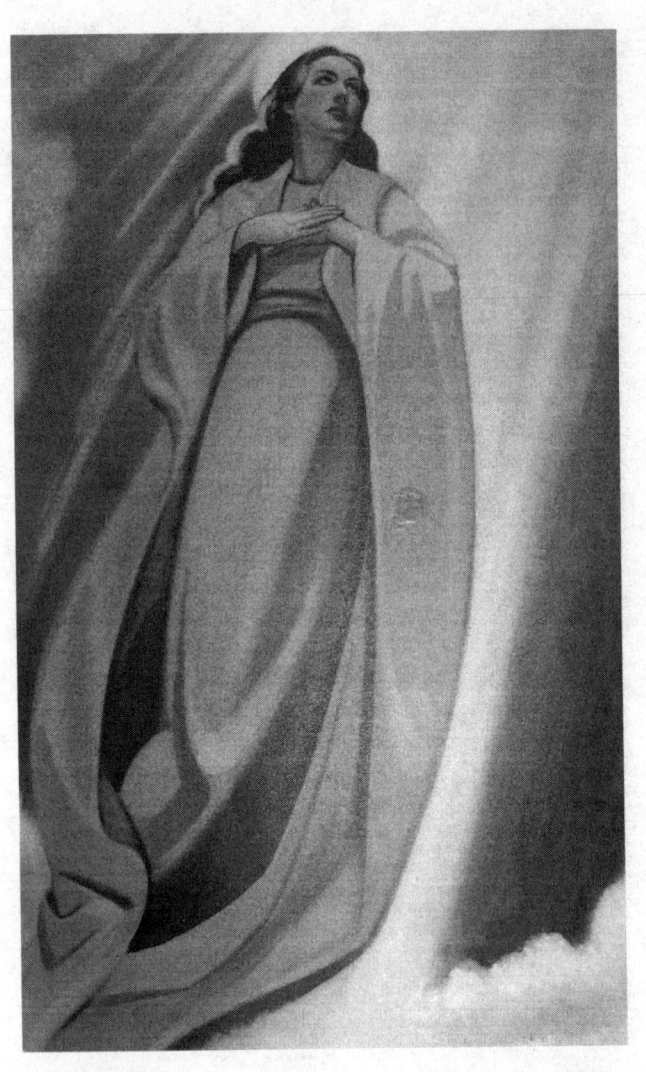

So, then, it was a tussle between Christian male and pagan female. The latter never really goes away, though. It might even be argued that the goddesses are back in force. There was one spotted not so long ago on Wandsworth

Common. What Martina could have added is that Brigid was also considered the goddess of poetry or what the ancient Irish deemed 'the flame of knowledge'. According to the Middle Irish collection *Lebor Gabála Érenn* (*The Book of the Taking of Ireland*), Brigid was herself a poet. Lady Gregory in *Gods and Fighting Men* (1904) describes her as 'a woman of poetry, and poets worshipped her, for her sway was very great and very noble. And she was a woman of healing along with that, and a woman of smith's work, and it was she first made the whistle for calling one to another through the night. And the one side of her face was ugly, but the other side was very comely. And the meaning of her name was *Breo-saighit*, a fiery arrow.' The Christian Brigid seems to have imported a good many pagan elements. According to the chronicler Giraldus Cambrensis, she was associated with the eternal sacred flame at Kildare, which was surrounded by a hedge. Any man attempting to cross the hedge would go insane and die, either that or his *dingle-twang* would wither. The fact too that the goddess Brigid was associated with hill-forts and fire would suggest that Martina's mind was unwittingly seared at an early age.

'The story about St Patrick driving the snakes from Ireland … when I was a child I was terrified of snakes. My first ever poem "There is a Snake in My Bed" was published in a swanky magazine called *Celtic Dawn*, edited by a man operating out of the Bee Gees' castle, in Thame, in Oxfordshire. Terence DuQuesne was some kind of Egyptologist and magic man who was friendly with Robin Gibb's Irish wife, Dwina, with whom he co-edited the magazine. My first experience of being published was being invited to the Bee Gees' castle. If I thought poetry was going to be sex, drugs and rock and roll, it was all downhill after that. Admittedly I got a funny feeling when the man at the drawbridge got on the telephone to Terence, "Put down that donkey, will you. Your visitor is here."'

And not only does that snake not go away, it grows in size too. A recent poem "Boa Constrictor" would suggest difficulties of an ophiological kind in County Cork. The 'big fat body of him', which Martina observes behind thick glass in the Dublin zoo, escapes. It is heading, as do so many of Martina's poems, towards a particular place.

> I saw the road from Dublin disappearing
> under his muscular body as he went past
> signposts, no need for such a diabolical fellow
> to check where he was going
> cleverly travelling at night, arranging himself
> carefully in ditches for sleep by day.
> Every so often, he might stop to open his mouth for
>   a sheep like
> the picture I'd seen in World Book Encyclopaedia.
> He knew where he was coming all right –
> the village of Burnfort.

All roads would seem to lead to Burnfort, which on the map remains invisible.

§

'What about life in the pub, shop and petrol pump?'
'My mother could never refuse anyone anything. People were always coming, begging for the last bit of whatever we had or else looking for drink.'

> Christmas Day and Good Friday
> were the only days that the pub closed.
> And yet they came –
> trembling strangers, under hats and caps,
> lapels turned up against the slanting wind
> or hiding a dog collar.

(from 'Desperate Men')

'She would be easily persuaded to give away her last bit of whatever it might be, often taking things out of the kitchen for people who knew they could work on her or even stuff that was not hers to give. Some people used to book their papers in advance, pay on yearly account. There was a local bachelor who took himself very seriously and would order the local papers, the *Cork Examiner* and the *Evening Echo*, and when he came he expected them to be there waiting for him. Invariably my mother would have given away one of the papers to someone else. "Oh, my God," she'd cry, "Christy Callaghan is coming!" We'd be sent flying out the back door to a neighbour with a two-shilling piece to buy back the newspaper and then somebody else would be out in the back kitchen, ironing it, straightening out the pages, and putting it together, and Christy, who'd experienced this one too many times before, would get all edgy. "Where's my newspaper?" he'd cry. "All I want is a drop of whiskey and my newspaper. Is it too much to ask for?" Sometimes it *was* too much to ask for. There were seventeen cats out back of the house … that's an approximate number because they came and went … and there was Fifi. My father wasn't allowed to feed them the best meat in the fridge. So I would aid and abet him. We had an electric meat slicer and I would watch out for him when he snuck in with a non-electric knife so as not to make any noise and he would be sawing away all these big chunks of meat which he would then run out to give to the cats. And because he'd be in such a rush the meat was left in a terrible condition and we couldn't sell it to anyone. Now I think of my poor mother but at the time I thought she was the arch-enemy of the cats. I don't think we had much business sense. Every now and then my mother would talk about the bailiffs coming. Somehow, though, they did manage. We were sent to boarding school, for instance.'

'And the publican side of things, what was that like?'
'Singing was a big thing when I was growing up but with the coming of TV and bands all that has died out. One person might have had a musical instrument but generally speaking people would just get up to do their party pieces and of course you knew what everyone's piece was going to be. I learned all the words to "Harper Valley PTA" and performed it. Do you know the lyrics? "Mrs. Johnson, you're wearing your dresses way too high. / It's reported you've been drinking and a-runnin' round with men and going wild." The customers would be thinking *what the hell*. I didn't know what it was about, but for sure it wasn't some lovely song about the IRA. Years later, someone in the bar said, "Ah, for the days when people sang!" and my older sister got really mad. "Oh, I remember them all right," she said. "*Bloody hell!* So-and-so would come down from the mountain and would have to sing his bit and we'd be all bored out of our heads and then Mr So-and-so would glare

at us while Mrs So-and-so sang, she who didn't have a note in her head, and, God, I'd be afraid to even touch a pint glass because Mr So-and-so would, like, give you such a vicious look." So you always had this other side to the lovely singsongs.'

'We were definitely considered oddballs. I think we had it in spades. My brother Tom was on his way to boarding school when he met a man on a train and the man said "Where are you from?" and Tom said "I'm from Burnfort" and the man said "Oh God, I *know* Burnfort. There is a pub there." And Tom opened his mouth to say he lived in the pub when the man continued, "Jesus, there is a funny family living in that pub. Do you know them?" And Tom said yes, and let the man talk away, entertain him all the way from Mallow Station to Limerick Junction on the foibles and eccentricities of the Cotter family. And then when Tom got up to change trains at Limerick Junction he said, "Before I go, I had better tell you I'm one of the funny ones." And he left the man with his jaw dropped down to his ankles.'

'It would seem literature came late to you.'

'It was *always* with me. I learned to read very young and that became my refuge. I was able to remove myself at the age of three. That's the irony of the whole thing: the end product of the reading is becoming a writer and *what* do I write about? All the things that I obviously *didn't* shut out despite having my head stuck in a book all the time. That's what it is, the fairy tale, the return in the myth. I got into a lot of trouble because we were always supposed to be minding the shop and the bar and the fact I was always reading was a bone of contention. There was one big row with some woman. I was rolling half a dozen oranges over the counter with my left hand while holding a book with my right hand, reading it. As a teenager I used to keep diaries which were just dire. I wish I'd kept them because they would be hilarious to read but they were really emotional and melodramatic. I tore them up because they disgusted me. I used to write out Maupassant stories in French, pretending they were mine. I can see now that this was a good way to learn to write and to this day if I really like a poem I'll write it out in longhand. It is like inhabiting it. You get a sense of its structure. But I wasn't thinking that at the time. I was just pretending to be Maupassant and very sophisticated because I was writing in French. So it was always there. Also my family were absolutely brilliant storytellers. My mother was always telling stories in public and in private. She'd drive us mad sometimes going off on tangents – free association, out of control – but sometimes the words and the way she said them was like a glove on the hand fitting just right. My sister Bernadette was very funny, with a great memory, and we would tell each other stories and like my mother she would be hungry for detail, asking exactly how people looked and asking me to repeat what they said and *how* they said it.'

'All this would appear to be connected to the very idea of Irishness, the gift of the gab.'

'And the feeling you *have* to entertain. I grew up with that. It was very much in the family. My mother would say, "Go down and talk to the customers", but with my head always stuck in a book I think I was hit and miss.'

'There is the boredom too, which in your writing acquires an almost mythic quality.'

'Yes, when boredom is heightened to a state of fascination, this is what art does. There is madness in it too. It is almost hysterical boredom.'

§

A growing strain in Martina's poetry, particularly in her most recent collection, *Facing the Public*, is Irish history, often the interstices in which it and family history become one. The poems, many of them imbued with what she calls the 'black note', are often told aslant, their revelations unintentional although that is precisely what they are meant to be. A boy suspected of informing for the Black and Tans is dragged by a horse and cart for forty miles, Ernie O'Malley of the IRA is given his say, and in prison her Uncle Tommy writes a letter about a grey mare, yearning for 'the day she'd come again / drumming her hooves'. Very rarely is anything spelled out in black and white. Martina shuns the propagandistic line. She brought out her family album of photographs, pausing at one, saying, 'We were doing a nativity play. I *think* I was the Virgin Mary.' As the photos moved from colour to monochrome, a history in reverse, the figures who flit in and out of her poems stared at me from their fixed places.

'These are my maternal grandparents. Her family refused to hang the picture because they didn't like *him*. Richard Cotter was very well-educated. Sometimes, when I hear stories about him with his moustache, I think of James Joyce's father, John. They were from roughly the same era and of the new rising Catholic middle class. Catholic Emancipation came in 1829. They'd both been to early Catholic boarding schools, John Joyce at St Colman's in Fermoy and Richard Cotter at St Michael's in Listowel. What I heard was that Richard Cotter was a silver-tongued devil and she, Elizabeth Cowhey, was a long-suffering woman with a lot of money. Look at that waist … it must have been uncomfortable … I wonder where her teeth are … she is keeping her mouth clammed shut … I have been to the dental museum in Wimpole Street and seen Victorian false teeth, wooden. Anyway I'm not going to go *there* … She and her sister, Mary, were followers of Parnell who haunts the pages of Joyce. They were big tenant farmers who got involved in Parnell's Land War campaign. This is going back to the late Victorian period and the beginning of the rise of the Catholic middle class. The plan of campaign was that the tenants would refuse to pay the landlords. You had to be brave. You would be evicted and then you would fight the eviction. It was decided that *she* would do it because she wouldn't get a long sentence like a man would. It would have been your typical eviction scene. All the windows on the first floor of the house were bricked up. She and her sister, Mary, went upstairs and they poured kettles of boiling water mixed with Indian meal down on the soldiers, the landlord, the bailiff, the battering ram, fixed bayonets. Eventually she was carried off to prison. When I visited Kilmainham Prison and inspected the various cells I discovered women weren't treated as political prisoners and that she would have been thrown in with the prostitutes. No one ever mentioned that! My mother, who really admired her, said she was a lady and that when she was in prison she refused to drink out of a tin mug and so they had to bring her a China cup and saucer. My mother also spoke of how she would darn socks for the workmen on the farm. Servants weren't often treated that well. As a child I was told she met Grandfather Cotter in prison. He had been imprisoned for cutting a rope bridge from under an RIC [Royal Irish Constabulary] man. One Sunday afternoon the RIC man was reclining on a rope bridge, watching the river and the minnows dancing in the sunlight off the water, and Richard Cotter snuck up on him, cut the ropes, and down went the RIC man among the minnows. That was his great blow for Irish freedom. Anyway there he was with his silver tongue and when they met apparently he didn't think all that much of her but after his release, when he found out she had three brothers all of whom died young and that she had ended up inheriting the farm, he hurried to Ballybunion where she convalescing at her aunt's hotel, courted her, and married her. Who knows for sure what happened? Economics are always a consideration and maybe people were more honest about mercenary motives back then. He was called "Ould Cotter" by some people and I remember being thrilled when I came across a character called Ould Cotter in *Dubliners*. My mother was the one who told me everything. Her voice goes right through those stories of the War of Independence. When she was growing up in the late 1920s she listened to those stories and soaked them up like a big piece of blotting paper. You would think she'd been there and actually witnessed the events. My poem "Two Hostages" is about my mother and my father being taken hostage, on separate occasions, by the Black and Tans, "one of them claiming that he couldn't *get over the brown eyes of the Irish*". My father never told me that story, my mother did.'

Martina turned another page in the album.

'Here's a lovely picture of Daddy and my Uncle Tommy in 1910, with their Eton collars. Daddy's on the right.'

'Why did your father go silent on all this history?'

'He was a quiet man. They were all traumatised. When he was dying of brain secondary all through the end he spoke about the Civil War – he was reliving it. That was even *less* spoken about. The Irish War of Independence *was* spoken about. It was a one-sided view of heroes, the *David and Goliath* thing, the IRA being David and the British Empire Goliath, and in a way it was, but it wasn't the *full* story. The Civil War, on the other hand, couldn't be discussed at all because it was too horrendous. My father was on Michael Collins's side. Somebody from the Republican side, a man called Cronin, shot the eye out of my father's uncle's head while he was shaving. Cronin's son became a politician and every time my father saw the election posters for him he'd start rumbling. We used to think it was hilarious when he and his friend Tom Twomey got all obsessed about the Civil War. We also teased them because we knew Michael Collins's followers became Blueshirts, quasi-fascists, with a uniform and – let me put it *this* way – a very distinctive salute. We poked fun at the Blueshirts, which wasn't very nice, but we didn't have much sympathy for their side of the Civil War. Some of them later went and fought with Franco.'

'Was your father involved in actual fighting?'

'Yes. He would have been very young though. That is all I know, he never spoke of it. I remember in the 1970s my brother came home drunk and said to him and his friend Tom Twomey, "You never said what the *other* side did. You never told us about Dirty Dick and 77 Republicans." Now, any mention of *that* was enough to start everyone off. General Richard Mulcahy, "Dirty Dick", would have been a hero of my father's. An ex-medical student when he joined the IRA, he was on Collins's side and then, during the Civil War, when he supported the Anglo-Irish Treaty, he executed 77 Republican prisoners. Tom Twomey used to smoke a pipe and drink by the fire. My father would be down there too, both of them quite old at this stage. They loved Fifi. When Tom Twomey came in he'd heat his flat cap in front of the fire to warm it up for Fifi who would jump into it and they would sit there admiring him, discussing the weather and talking about old times. So when my brother came in that night, shouting at them about Dirty Dick and the 77, they went berserk. These old men who would never say boo to a goose held him up against the wall. My sister Bernadette who was there told me Tom Twomey's false teeth were clacking with temper.'

'Those are the details I love!'

§

The time had come to shift houses.

'Listen,' she said, 'do you see the chandelier?'

I stared up at the ceiling of the not-quite-*Ulysses*-blue room in the house opposite the boarded-up front of the Turkish library on Balls Pond Road.

'I got it for fifteen quid from a street trader in Camden Passage – he got it in a house clearance in the East End. It's art deco. I grew up in a scrap merchant's house that was full of salvage, the ship's panelling, for example, and poetry for me is another form of salvage, salvage from the wreckage. And this, too, in more ways than one, is a bit of salvage. There are iron bars from Clerkenwell Prison upstairs. I dream of houses all the time. They are wonderful dreams because I keep finding more rooms that I never knew I had. Freud said the psyche is like a house. One of the first things young children draw is a house.'

These houses grow inside us.

I dreamt of a house in Holloway
in a circle of mountains,
a green ocean washing the front door.

My daughter talks
of a house with a stream
running right through the middle,
the Salmon of Knowledge
lepping for joy inside.

(from 'Dream Houses')

'I think *this* is my dream house. Lately I'm dreaming more of gardens. I dream of there being more to my garden, sunny spots I never knew I had, and in them I'm planting roses and fuchsias. If there is any religion that comes to me I think it is through gardening, the magic of things growing, dying and coming back. I don't think it matters *how* we come back. I've been dreaming too about the garden in Burnfort and that makes me so happy because I feel close to my mother like I was when I was a child. I was mad about her then, and with everyone else away at school we'd be close. One dream sounds gruesome. I am kneeling, planting roses, but instead of a box of bone meal beside me there is a corpse and I am breaking bits off it to put in with the roses as fertiliser. In the dream I'm happy though and maybe it's a metaphor for writing because I believe we write for the dead.'

Martina is, arguably, the noisiest woman to have ever laid siege to a kitchen. She sliced red peppers for her famous red pepper soup, the clanging of pots and pans and the higher notes of spoons and knives, together creating a din through which, on the recording I made, I struggle hard to follow her words. She then put on the rice.

What's missing from the image is the knife she was holding when I suggested she might not be quite the feminist she believes she is. I only narrowly missed being added to the peppers. What I think I really meant to say is that she is uncontainable. There's no ideology that'll keep her in one place.

Martina came to London in 1988 and worked for some years as a radiographer. When I remarked on how masculine nurses' uniforms had become we embarked on a strange disquisition that might have had something to do with the connectivity of form and appearance.

'I can't ever bear to talk about the deterioration of the nurses' uniforms these days! Those awful trouser suits, and there's no sign any more of those lovely big headdresses for the Sisters in Charge. I weep when I think of what is gone. I think the uniforms were very beautiful. A part of me hates all that hierarchy but for me it had glamour, an element of safety. I suppose I'm not being practical as trousers are more comfortable. I'd love it if they brought back the Latin Mass too, but as I wouldn't go to church anyway I'm not entitled to complain. I had an experience once, which makes me think of the Circe episode in Joyce, where all these masochistic events happen to Leopold Bloom. That was the thing about James Joyce – he wasn't ashamed to show those aspects of himself – the humiliation, the masochistic bits, all the hallucinatory stuff that goes on in the brothel – he showed every side of the human being. And that's what's so hard about being a writer, what one has to reveal about oneself. Anyway I was with a friend in the King's Head in Islington. We were deep in conversation and alcohol. I have a bad sense of direction and instead of going downstairs to the toilet I went upstairs and entered a dressing room which I didn't know was there. A World War I British soldier – they obviously had some play on – appeared in the room, absolutely incensed, and he obviously wasn't going to get out of character for me. I can't remember what he said but I remember backing out of the room. Perhaps he was enjoying himself, I don't know.'

'Could it be you interrupted a performance?'

'I hope to God not, but I remember getting great pleasure out of the whole thing, after the initial fright, *definitely* in recounting it. Whatever he looked like, now, in my imagination, he is six foot six, blond, wearing a pale khaki uniform. Also he had on these puttees, or if he didn't he has them on now. He's in one of my novels in progress. You remember the girl in my novel *No Drinking, No Dancing, No Doctors* steals a nurse's uniform. When I was a child I wanted one and I liked being in hospitals the few times I was in them – the clean sheets, the nurses with their upside-down watches, those lovely pillbox hats and the strange curvy veils. The thing about wearing a uniform was that I felt I was playing a role. A hospital is, after all, a dramatic place. I don't mean melodramatic but what Robert Frost meant when he said everything is as good as it is dramatic.'

It was here, in London, soon after her father died, she began to write. It was here she gave birth to her daughter and it was here that her marriage fell to pieces. And it was here, at the time when the courts were determining whether to overturn the judgements on certain people accused of bombings in the 1970s, that she felt the need to acquaint herself more with Irish history.

'Those were still highly political times because of reopening of the Birmingham Six and Guildford Four cases. I'd walk into the staff room at the hospital and people would be saying terrible things about them, what I call "tabloid comments". I didn't really know that much about Irish history and I hadn't been very political, or, if so, only through what my mother told me. Still I couldn't believe people were so ill-informed and could make such ignorant statements about what was happening. I began to try to explain to them about Ireland but they didn't understand. They called me "the IRA". It was hard being called that. One man I worked with, whenever a bomb went off, would ring me up wherever I was and say, as a joke, "Where were you last night?" I was in my twenties then, in my nurse's uniform. I think I've been trying to explain Ireland ever since. What I'm really interested in, though, are people who don't have a voice. This is especially true of the Irish who came here before me, as labourers, who John McGahern called "the silent generation". I became fascinated with all those builders and labourers because I used to X-ray them at the Whittington. These were men who came over in the 1950s whereas my generation came over with more education and confidence. They were incredibly sad and touched something inside me. I was looking back through them to my parents who were very unhappy as immigrants, who had been well-off farmers, middle-class with servants, and suddenly ended up in Australia where they were like the rest of the paddies.'

The stories of those Irish who came to England in the 1950s have been captured most poignantly in Catherine Dunne's *An Unconsidered People – The Irish in London* (2003). She describes them as having become 'doubly invisible' in both their own and their adopted countries. The more Martina delves into her country's past, the more she becomes a conduit for what she calls the 'black note'.

'There is this fantastic book, *The Burning of Bridget Cleary*, which is so compassionate, so empathic and so informative. She was an Irish woman burnt to death by her husband in a fireplace in 1895. They thought she was a fairy. It was a bad time for this to happen. The Unionists had a field day of it, saying, "We can't allow these savages Home Rule." One of the things that really interested me as a writer was the court evidence. There had been a local fairy doctor, somebody else giving advice, various relations standing around and doing nothing to stop this man who'd obviously gone out of his head. The strangest story! They were all in court now and the people there, depending on whether they were pre-famine or post-famine, gave very different evidence. Those who had been born before the Great

Marius Kociejowski: Once Upon a Time in County Cork

Famine were generally illiterate while those born after it were literate. The people who'd been to school gave expositions in which they simply related what happened, but when the illiterate people got up in the witness box they went into complete dramatic mode. They recreated and visualised the whole thing for themselves. The best writers are people who can do *that*. A lot of people can't visualise and what they relate just won't come alive. The reason why I'm interested in *voice* is because it often chooses the black note. Neruda has it in his "Ode to Death". I can't *explain* the black note. You know it when you hear it and the Irish have a lot of it, with their love of funerals. They relish it. It's what Joyce has in *Ulysses*. The most powerful voice there is Stephen Dedalus who is based on Joyce's father, John, who is from Cork, who is malicious, witty, funny, dark, coarse ... an incredible voice that jumps off the page. So much writing comes from the dead. I started writing after my father died. As I said before, I think we write for the dead, we inhabit their voices. Yeats talks about how the dead have wisdom but no power ... we have the power and the dead try to make us do their bidding. I don't want to merely repeat what Lorca says about *duende*, but this is why I like the dramatic monologue, when people are unconscious of what they reveal about themselves, hang themselves in speech or whatever. Voices are at their most powerful when admitting the dark in themselves to someone else. A really bland example of this would be somebody launching into conversation with "I am not a racist" and then goes on to demonstrate otherwise. I tried to do this particularly in the monologues "Reprisal" and "The Boy from Durras" where the people speaking give an account of what has happened – a terrible dark thing, revenge. You know how in tragedy there is a cathartic sense, a sense of completeness, that this is what life is about, and the voice has a satisfaction, almost enjoyment, about it even as it is telling you something terrible. It is like someone grabbing you by the collar and saying, "Yes, this is what it's like. Have a look." I think most of the time poetry can deal with dark subjects much better than fiction. It can deal with torture, the Holocaust, and compared to it fiction doesn't even come near. It is closer to prayer, on a higher register soundwise. That's why I never like fiction as much because there is an element of judging that goes on, which does not go into poetry. I always felt very exposed when writing fiction because it is about arranging people. You give your view on people, on how they act, on how they talk to each other, on how they react, and that shows how you see people. That makes me feel far more naked than if I revealed a secret about myself such as I'd killed or robbed someone. I do not judge people when I'm writing poetry. If writing is to do with the relationship between the writer and the reader, the reader finishing what the writer starts, then I think in most fiction it's the writer who finishes it. It's for that reason poetry is more healing to write. It allows us to release some of the darkness in ourselves. I think that's how *duende* comes into people's speech, which is why the story of Bridget Cleary really fascinated me because here were people who sat about, churning milk or whatever, while a woman was burnt to death and they were all thinking to themselves, "Oh, no" or "Go easy on her there." You can see how jealousy, resentment, fear and cowardice allowed this thing to happen. This can happen in any situation no matter what it is – it could be the Rosenbergs in the United States getting executed. There is a play called *The Little Foxes* by Lillian Hellmann, where the servant says something about there being people who eat the world and those who stand around and watch them eating the world.'

'You say it took your leaving Ireland to enable you to write ...'

'You can't go back!'

'But you do so all the time in your work.'

'Yes, but still you can't go back physically and even if I did there'd be nothing to return to. The pub is rented out, there's no post office in the village. There isn't even a shop any more. It really is a vanished world. I do think you lose something else. You become more of a foreigner there and you are one here as well. Although I'm in a very different situation, I am an exile.'

'You consider yourself so, an exile as opposed to an émigrée?'

'The word seems to me the right one.'

'As someone *forced* out of Ireland?'

'On a realistic level that sounds totally self-indulgent but I think I'm telling the truth. The word *sounds* right to me, as if the sound *is* the sense. I suppose self-imposed exile ... I felt I needed to get away to write.'

'So the years of being here haven't lessened your sense of being an exile?'

'I never entered the Irish *thing* because I don't go to church. I have always felt like an outsider. You know something – the first place where I felt I belonged ... I was 28 at the time ... was the Torriano Meeting House. There I met the wonderful John Rety and a lot of eccentric people. I recited a poem from the floor. There was a man with a can of beer, holding a dog by a string, sitting on the edge of the stage, very unnerving, and there I was shaking, reading out my first poem. And then he asked me to read it again! But, to go back to your question, I think one responds to the deepest tribal parts of oneself. Edna O'Brien says the exiled writer is joined by a cable to his native country. But then I love being here because I'm free. It is a great escape from who you are. Coming here started me writing as much as my father's death did. My sister Mary brought me here for a week's holiday when I was eleven and I completely fell in love with the place. I have always been in love with London. I think for me it is having this safe little place within the city, my own little microcosm, and then I make little forays out into the jungle. The garden feels like a secret too. *The Secret Garden* was another favourite childhood book, another book of divination. I lie in the hammock under the honeysuckle at the bottom of the garden ... and it's a secret ... the blackbirds are singing ... the cats are around me ... and at the same time I hear the roar of the traffic and the police sirens ... peace and noise all at the same time. Also for me the world of books was London. I felt I had come to the right place.'

There was a slightly acrid, black smell in the air. Suddenly there was a panicked look in Martina's eyes.

'I think I've burned the rice,' she cried. 'Isn't that terrible?'

'Yes,' I said, 'and at this stage in life too.'

ANNE STEVENSON
Two Poems

The Master and his Cast
A tribute to Henry James

Passing first class on their luxury liner through the straits
Of the nineteenth and twentieth centuries, they lingered on deck
In dinner jackets and jewelled gowns, looking perhaps like advertisements
For expensive perfume, but playing for possession of the sunset.
Fortunes steamed over the sea to them, waiters in black raced between them
Bearing trays of iced syrup and soda-water, while at ease
In the narrows of their ways, he steered them through a channel of lawns
Green as billiard tables, shaded by porticos and elm trees –
Beauty at its cruellest most civilised at Matcham and Fawns.
Justice settled which girls would be turned into monsters,
Which would suffer victory to vindicate innocence. Yes, wealth
Does a great deal to worry goodness in those late magniloquent chapters,
More art than odyssey, more parable than myth;
But why should a gilded tour of betrayal not feature privilege and princes?
Beyond the next rock lay the wreck. It moves me to think of him
Scrupulously analysing Scylla right there on the lip of Charybdis.

Vince, getting on with his life

'Hey! That's Vince,'
I said,
or almost said,
as a lean, bald patch
loped past me up our hill,
and I recognised,
or thought I did,
the joker on the window sill
(he fit the frames and fixed the latch)
with whom I, laughing,
used to chat,
not meaning anything
by talking
but 'Let's be friendly!'
i.e. that
being two,
and being human,
we maybe had
as much in common
as wagging dogs
or jackdaws larking.

It might have been
the tilted angle of his head
he carried low
to hide his face,
or how his work-stained
back expressed
some jokeless trouble
made him seem
less like the Vince
I used to know,
more like his double
or his ghost,
or worse,
a self-accusing dream
out of my own experience.
I had to hesitate.
I didn't say hello.
Why did I wait
till – watching him
run to his boss's van
and clamber in –
it was too late?

DON COLES
Two-Hander

To my newborn grandson

There was usually a warning. 'If you're
So set on it,' my Gramp would be told, 'go ahead.
But keep in mind he's just a little boy.'
That was Gran. While she was talking
He'd be studying whatever piece of wall
He was nearest to, or adjusting his hat,
The straw one with the black band
Around the bottom of the crown. Then
Out the cottage's back door we'd both go,
Him carrying the two-hander.

It was shaped like a harp. This is
Seventy years later, a long while for
A simile's slow glow to be mounting
Towards a page's, this one's, surface, but
The saw's shape never wavered.
It hung on pegs on the wall in
The entry-way, and only came down
Once or twice a summer.

The simile's stronger for the wait.

Its wooden handles were painted crimson,
A dried-blood colour, as I now realise.
They were the smoothest things of wood
I've ever held. My hands clench,
Remembering them.

He didn't say much, my Gramp. But
I'd catch him watching me
When we were out there, the two of us
Standing in a pine-tree wood
On a yellowing pine-needle floor, and
Along with the watching there'd sometimes be
An awkwardness in him, something unsure or shy,
Glimpses of all those, which may just have been
What could he do about the years,
So many of them, such a jumble when he turned to
Look back – the imbalance between us that
Words wouldn't fix. And meanwhile
My arms would be stretching out towards him
When the saw moved in that direction,
And then they'd be pushed back until they were
Almost behind me, and then further forward again,
And everything repeating.

When the log started to tilt downwards at
Its middle, meaning it was about to break into
Its two new halves, you had to stop right away
And lift the blade up and out. I'd probably have
Taken my T-shirt off by then, and now I'd
Pick it up and throw it over my shoulder.
We'd walk to the stream where, years and years
Ago, he'd stuck a V-shaped length of tin tightly
Among the stream-bed's stones. A small saucepan
Was half-hidden among the weeds and he'd fill this
From the water running as from a tap out of
The front of the V-shaped tin. He'd watch
The water settle and clear in his pan and then
Drink all he wanted and rinse the pan out before
Passing it to me. I'd do what I'd watched him do.

All this comes from the two-handed saw which
I'm remembering as much of as I can, only
Because of you, little one, resting among us
In your dream of Eden, and a lot smaller
Than I was then, whose dream never showed
The two of us in a wood together, as we will never be.

ADRIAN MAY

The Hang of Song

ARCTIC MONKEYS, *Suck It and See* (Domino Recordings) £10
CLARE POLLARD, *Changeling* (Bloodaxe Books) £8.95

The borders between song and poetry are often argued over, even if historically and at some deeper level they do not really exist. In 'The Music of Poetry' (1942), T.S. Eliot insists that this music is not merely rhythm or metre, but also 'is not something that exists apart from the meaning'. If the music and the meaning are one, then the song aspect of poetry is not easily dismissed, nor vice versa, as it is such a primal aspect of the energy of both. When, in the same essay, Eliot outlines the tendency of poetry to need to return towards common speech and to form, we might be reminded of two things popular song takes for granted, establishing a further connection. Comparing a poet and a songwriter who show and work against some of these connections might then be fruitful, especially when they also seem concerned, as Eliot confesses he is, with what you can do with your talent and promise, with trying 'to formulate' what you want 'to write'.

I don't know if there is such a thing as fourth album/collection syndrome, but all that is subsequent to early promise risks dashing expectations. Metaphorically we participate in this myth, whereby we hope the artist might model our own promise and hope. Arctic Monkeys' fourth album has been eagerly searched by critics for a prodigal return to the early form of their first album *Whatever People Say I Am, That's What I'm Not*, made when singer/lyricist Alex Turner was still a teenager. Clare Pollard's fourth collection of poems comes from a similar situation of early promise, her first, *The Heavy-Petting Zoo*, having been published when she was still at school. How do you go on, sustain, maintain, renew and not get upstaged by your own loud, chiming lyrical innocence – except by retaining that innocence in an experiential way, finding the poetry in the songs and the songs in the poetry, which is what these two writers do? So Alex Turner sings, in 'Library Pictures', 'Trust some ellipses to chase you round the room / Through curly straws and metaphors and goo', while Clare Pollard, in 'Broadstairs', writes, 'By snapping, smashing, spuming sea, / this beast will make a song of me'. Already, we can see them playing with their forms, in a muscular and shape-shifting way, as rehearsed in both their slippery titles. There is a defiant energy and wit in both and a desire not to be contained or restrained by what they do with their giftedness.

Both, then, are bristling with verbal energy and show no diminution in talent or productivity. The one thing they have learned is that you cannot try to repeat your innocence, however knowing or complex it might have been. You have to move into songs of experience, so as not to ossify, and both have passed this test. Things tend to get more complex and self-reflective, which is not always a good thing, or even a good subject, and while both deal with this, they do it in different ways. Alex Turner plays with the form and content of the pop song, while pledging himself to it in a wittily disingenuous way: 'I poured my aching heart into a pop song / I couldn't get the hang of poetry', he says in the title track, following this with 'That's not a skirt girl it's a sawn off shotgun / And I can only hope you've got it aimed at me'. This is Alex doing poetry, after having just said he can't, while reasserting the comic sexy sparkle of his earlier poppiness. His acceptance of himself as lyricist with poetic leanings is reinforced by the fact that the CD booklet contains his printed words for the first time.

The sex and mystery of the title song 'Suck It and See', as quoted above, make it a good example of Alex Turner's recent work, in which the poetic wit, while present, is playing with variations of repulsion and attraction. The frivolity is part of the charm and tease, but at times only the best bits get beyond their surface paradox. Popular love song can have its poetic obscurity too, but it sometimes feels here like a refuge from meaning, rather than a quest for something new.

'Reckless Serenade' seems aware of this problem. It begins with the usual mystery dance but ends with him questioning himself in the chorus: 'I've been trying to figure out / exactly what it is I need / Called up to listen to the voice of reason but got his answering machine'. Hence he is still singing about 'singing a reckless serenade'. This is both self-conscious and self-questioning, as well as questioning the form he works in. He reminds you of his capacity while attempting to reach beyond it.

The most convincing of these post-love songs lyrically is 'Love is a Laserquest', in which a reflective, retrospective mood can speak of the loved one 'breaking hearts with the efficiency / that only youth can harness', as he wonders whether he can continue 'pretending you were just some lover'. The subtlety of the form and self-questioning has an overlay of real insight: 'I've tried to ask you this is some daydreams that I've had / but you're always busy being make believe'.

Clare Pollard is, on the surface, less interested in delving into self-consciousness via form. While she binds herself to poetic changeability, it is to the purpose of making a song of herself via traditional forms of ballad, folklore and storytelling. Here she manages to combine the raw energy of her confrontational, confessional work with the dark, mythically challenging ache of the old tales. She gets, therefore, a kind of doubled effect of dark themes becoming deeper in a proper combination of energy and maturity. Grasping the world of experience, then, is in her title and her first poem 'Tam Lin's Wife', where the motive is holding on to the shape-shifting husband, whatever the change, like a Proteus who will finally give the answer. The poem is finally about holding on to love, but could also be an image of the poetry of a persistent attention to experience and the changes mythic material helps us adapt to. The energy of the Child collection ballad source-song is thus turned to a positive poetic, as well as a powerful love song which confronts its experience, even when the good things seem 'stripped off one by one', as the poem says. Here she builds on, rather than plays with, her prodigy work of raw, personal force.

This opening poem then stands as a manifesto or fanfare for the whole collection, as it gradually moves towards the form and meaning of its origin. It starts unrhymed, but by the final few lines a triple rhyme emerges from the mist and rings out, its last word an emphatic beat: 'and love has no conditions. None.' Her new poetic form, or self, has happened. There is an exuberance here, in subject and in the art, of embracing new forms and experiences.

The difference then, in a surprising way, is that while Alex Turner is arguing with the formal constraints via his ironies and mysteries, Clare Pollard, from her earlier confessional and raw work, has no history of irony to fall back on. If she is self-conscious, it might only be when the intensity seems a bit automatic. In the major poems here, such as 'Reynardine', 'The Two Ravens' and 'The Skulls of Dalston', she is able to connect the serious, contemporary ambition of her early work to the strong meat of the ballad. Her mysteries are more productive.

Alex Turner, meanwhile, in an edition of the BBC 2 music show *Later* (May 2011), sang more ironic takes on song from the album, interspersed with songs from Randy Newman, the grandpa of lyric ironies, which made the connection between their approaches palpable. Newman, whose songs often speak in the voices of the prejudiced ('Short people got no reason to live', for instance), seemed a natural relative to Alex Turner's 'What you waiting for? / Sing another fucking shalala', from 'The Hellcat Spangled Shalalala'. This song is probably the most extreme mystery/irony interrogation of his craft on the album.

Still five years younger than Clare Pollard, Alex Turner might learn from her to re-inhabit the narrative power of song, seemingly so easily attained on the Monkeys' first album, with its tales of one weekend. If there is a theme to *Suck It and See*, it is one of experiential uncertainty, as revealed in the last verses and lines of the album, as well as in the comically mocking title of the single 'Don't Sit Down 'Cause I've Moved Your Chair'. 'That's Where You're Wrong' adds some weight to the questioning: 'You're not the only one / That time's got it in for ... There are no handles you can hold / And no understanding where it goes'.

In 'Thirtieth', Clare Pollard writes about what Alex Turner might have been thinking of, Sandy Denny's song 'Who Knows Where The Time Goes'. This poem might be playing with her earlier persona, who feels, like the speaker in 'That's Where You're Wrong', the unease of growth: 'My friends, we are so lucky and so disgusting, / and will pay for this tomorrow.' This shared, ominous note comes, though, not at the end like Alex Turner's, but in the midst of poems that confront change and hope so fruitfully. Her final poem even confronts the self-consciousness of turning to earlier, folky song-models, where, on a Romany caravan holiday, 'hired to imagine us gipsies', the imaginings and reality of facing 'the chill wind' results in an achieved liberation: 'blasting away our mortgage, / emails, bills, TV, our broken washing machine'. She embraces change again, as in her opening poem, via the hang of song, singing the fear that hangs bravely into the positive.

This final poem, 'The Caravan', thus challenges her new persona and reinforces the sense of an intelligent combination of the traditional in contemporary form, as recommended by T.S. Eliot, of course. She is, like Alex Turner, questioning her whole being, in the confessional way, while connecting that with the tests and trials of the untamed forms and themes. The rhyming is there and the nomadic quest/holiday of poetry is called on and found pertinent and potent, with the holiday a test of the old truth against the new. Here the fire works: 'It kindled and started to lick, and you laughed'.

At its best, Arctic Monkeys' album makes the same kind of testing leap into the elemental. 'If you're gonna try and walk on water / make sure you wear your comfortable shoes', as 'Piledriver Waltz' tells us. In a way, the counter to accepted differences applies when comparing songs and poems. Poems have to have an instant appeal through the words, not having the time or setting to breathe through music. They tend also to become more condensed and processed than songs, as well as longer. The task for the poet is then to remain song-like, despite these innate disadvantages, while the task of the songwriter is to pack in the poetry without allowing it to get in the way of the looser and shorter formal constraints. If song is the primal form, then the hang, the formal promise and the danger, might be in catchiness, in the sense of how it sings in the mind, but also how it catches and transforms the experiential. Both writers here achieve that in their own ways and forms, but while Arctic Monkeys are playing with their promise, often to great and always verbally exciting effect, Clare Pollard is singing away with exemplary strength and purpose. Both are catchy, celebratory, sexy, funny, intense, verbally exuberant, mocking, good at titles, and shocking and raw, but we believe Clare Pollard when she says she is 'no longer afeart', in 'Waiting for the Kettle to Boil, Lancashire', and, as if to song itself, 'I've tales to tell and am brimming with love / for what brought me to love'.

JANET KOFI-TSEKPO
Six Poems

Beginnings

When we were hungry
we tore the waves
and pulled out fish,

enough to feed a family
of seals. The raw flesh
excited us. We hunted

for more on land,
rabbits and voles,
ripped goats' heads

from bristling necks.
We watched the birds
and navigated the air

with wood and bone.
At times, we wore
the skins of beasts.

Odin

My moon eye floats
in Mimir's well –

I have drunk deep
from his pool.

I have hung myself
upon Yggdrasil

to learn the secrets
of the dead.

I have used my spear
on the battle bed.

I am blood spilled
on the apple tree,

flesh on the wolf's
frosted teeth.

This is an axe-age,
a sword-age,

but a new land rises
from the sea.

Psalm

Hand, work slow,
break the clouds like bread,
let rain fall like wine,

let rivers flow
with fish, water the vine.
Hand, work slow.

Cross

On this tree, I have broken
into a star – at each point
bitter, salty, pungent,
sour. Now a sweetness
melts on the tongue
like a life remembered.

The Arch

I have seen this arch before;
the short tunnel leading to water.
My feet were coated with dust,
that is the last thing I remember.
Just a few weeks earlier, we had
killed a goat and were celebrating
the end of the rainy season.
Suddenly, two of my cousins
took me by the legs – I thought
they were joking – and then
I became aware of the deadness
in their eyes, and was frightened.
I soon found myself underground.
The smell of soot and blood
made my nose jump around
like an ugly demon. Too many things
I cannot mention happened there.
But now I could see, nudged
by the bitter wind that blew in
from the Sahara, a very large hut
floating on water, the clothes
of a giant master hanging out to dry.

Havana

Little rocking bird
in your silver pod
under the palms

in the conservatory –
with whom did you speak,
and why is that beak

so still today?
Brighter than
the cars lined up

beside the Hotel
Nacional; brighter
than the washed

stone slums nestling
together like
carefully planted seeds.

CAROL RUMENS

In Conversation with Maurice Rutherford

CAROL RUMENS: *Who were the first poets whose work was important to you?*

MAURICE RUTHERFORD: Among the anthologies I found in the public library was *The Oxford Book of Twentieth-Century English Verse*, chosen by Philip Larkin. Some of the contents were such a revelation to me that I wanted to own a copy. This was the first poetry book I ever bought – the first of many. Perhaps it was to be expected that I should start by reading the poets of around my generation. But, although I share Larkin's year of birth, his poems were not the first to capture my attention, but those dealing with World War II experiences, poems by Charles Causley, Keith Douglas, Vernon Scannell and especially Henry Reed, whose 'Naming of Parts' showed me a picture from my own life as an eighteen-year-old virgin recruit being introduced to the Lee Enfield rifle whilst daydreaming of other things (not least of all, sex). I was made suddenly aware that deeply moving poems could be written about life as I knew or had known it.

Before discovering earlier poets such as Edward Thomas and Thomas Hardy I found the work of another Thomas, a Welshman writing in English, and it was with him that I first experienced 'hearing' the music of poetry lifting from the printed page, the music of language so beautiful that I couldn't not thrill to it; a beauty to bring tears. It is to R.S. Thomas I feel the most indebted.

Do you write naturally in form? I am interested in everything you have to say about form, line-breaks, stanza-structure!

Yes, I do find it helps if I aim to observe certain rules and boundaries when I'm thinking a poem onto the page. Could it possibly go back over the years to classroom initiation into regular, even monotonous, quatrains in what I was never taught were iambics? Maybe. Certainly now that I'm conscious of these matters I find myself easily *thinking* in iambic pentameter and sometimes when writing a poem I even fight against its regularity and am pleased when a word occurs whose length or stress introduces variety. I find the sonnet in particular helps me concentrate, rather than dilute, expression of the original thought. When I was a soldier, I found the footdrill on the barracks square, once the commands and movements were mastered, became second nature; simply follow orders and you were safe. You 'had it cushy'. Perhaps any reluctance to go walkabout and experiment is rooted in the fear of producing what is called, sometimes justifiably, chopped-up prose rather than the hoped-for exciting free verse which can use line-break, enjambment, original stanza structure, print layout, etc., to add emphasis, a contrary flow of thought, change of mood or texture, to bring the poem to life in the reader's mind. I am not sure. But I do thrill to this kind of brave, deep-sea-going, close-to-the-wind work of other poets when well written.

Looking back over my work, I am pleased to see poems which *have* moved a little beyond the constraints I feel more comfortable with. I am conscious that formal style, if rigidly adhered to, demands a very high quality in all the other ingredients of the poem if it is not to invite comparison with painting-by-numbers. But yes, in advancing years I'm pleased to have the support of the sonnet as my trusty zimmer frame.

In those very early experiences of poetry, the 'regular, even monotonous quatrains' of the classroom, did any poems make an impression on you? Do you remember any poems by heart?

The first 'school' poem to make a lasting impression on me was read, during morning assembly, I think, by the headmaster at my elementary school; its title was 'The Enchanted Shirt'. What surprised me as a young lad was that such an austere, unapproachable man as Mr Craven was seen to be could find pleasure in a poem about a beggar rolling around on the grass and laughing 'till his face was black', and that he so obviously relived that pleasure by sharing it with an audience, albeit a captive one! I would come to look back on his enjoyment as a gift. It was later, in secondary school English lessons, that the repetitive quatrains began to plough their furrows and, yes, I can still recite by heart the opening stanzas of Thomas Gray's 'Elegy written in a Country Churchyard'.

What motivated you to choose the 'Whitsun Weddings' stanza for your poem 'The Autumn Outings'? Was it a difficult poem to write, technically, or in any other sense?

The poem 'The Whitsun Weddings' must have been occupying my mind for about twelve years. I had read it many, many times, always fascinated by Larkin's ability to add a further layer to the imagery of a preceding line, his fluent syntax, his unobtrusive rhyme-scheme, the storyteller's gift taking me deeper into the subject than I'd have expected, and the boldness of the unusual four-syllable second line maintained throughout the stanzas. And yet, much as I enjoyed and admired the poem, something disturbed me. Could it be that I saw this as another of those poems presented through the eyes of an onlooker into the lives of others?

Perhaps it comes down mostly in the end to that old fiddler-on-the-roof, class-consciousness. The majority of great and/or popular poets writing in English during the past couple of centuries, Larkin among them, came from very comfortably-off backgrounds. These privileged poets benefited from years spent in the company of tutors/mentors, from access to libraries of great works, from time to read and to practise their art. It's no more surprising that they should be the ones to write eloquently than that they chose sometimes to write about those unfortunates who lacked the literacy authentically to chronicle their own lives.

I, certainly, couldn't even think, let alone write, in the manner of these masters. But maybe I could attempt to put on record something of the emotions common among the rank-and-file – those wedding parties 'from banquet-halls up yards' – descendants perhaps of Goldsmith's 'bold peasantry' – with the weddings over and back in their working or jobless environment, which had also been my own? Yes, muck or nettles, I'd have a go! I'd steal from, and at the same time pay homage to, Larkin by using the stanza-form and rhyme-scheme of his 'Whitsun Weddings' and try to bounce a few phrases of my own off memorable ones of his.

Deciding what to leave out would have presented the hardest problems. I don't keep records – or drafts, of which there'd be getting on for twenty – but I remember being absorbed throughout three full weeks before the poem was finished or, as Auden – I think it was – suggested, 'abandoned'.

When you begin a poem, do you generally already have a sense of its form, or does the form evolve slowly, or even suddenly reveal itself near the end?

Beginning a poem? You've got me at once excited and scared at the thought! Oh, dear. Well, it varies. Sometimes I have ideas for a poem, but no inkling of what form it might take. It's as if I'm shuffling through the shag-pile under horse-chestnut trees, hoping to uncover the bright blink of maroon I can pick up and string together with the conker or two I already have. Serendipity. Sometimes a battle of wills develops between a preconceived form and the phrases I'm trying to mould into shape. At other times a thought presents itself in the shape of a line which seems ready-made and unalterable, from which a pattern quickly builds up with very little effort on my part, and a poem may result.

MAURICE RUTHERFORD

Heinz Gropsmeyer

Almost forty years and your name still moves,
shrapnel under the skin, on reflective days.
You were not much older then than in the *Wehrmacht*
photograph above your name, twenty to my twenty-two.
Your canvas pack told more of you – *Kölnisswasser*,
talcum, *Rotbart* blades – though you had not lain
long enough to grow death's beard. More the lad
down someone's street than hated Hun or Boche
the jackboots made of you.

I tried to pull off the boots, not to ease
your stiff feet but perhaps to please mine
or strip the camouflage from common fundamentals.
I had heard, in school, of your brown shirt,
summer camp and sung-devotion to the Fatherland;
in your new fieldgrey, singing your *Horst Wessel* song
could you have known that we, too, paraded colours
into church for blessing of the same *Gott*
you wore on your buckled belt?

And what of your comrades; he of your own age
unable to rise from his roadside splint, lifting
only his head, inches from my advancing tank,
lest the last bone of blood-let youth be crushed?
And who was he, ageing, who ran through the vineyard
where Charlie took aim, life – and a sickness too?
I remember only his greylined face – and the change
in Charlie – but did not learn his name like yours.

Not a month later an ambulance driver
called the likes of you and me lucky
son-of-a-goddamn-bitches to get up the front,
and offered to trade his Ronson for my belt that was yours.
The belt I later gave away with other spoils of war
but not your name, Heinz Gropsmeyer; it stayed on.
I think of us now, there where you took your *Abschied*,
green grapes under the searing *mezzogiorno* sun;
shrapnel shifting in a distant vineyard's tilth.

Maurice Rutherford: Heinz Gropsmeyer

NEIL POWELL
Four Poems

Proof of Identity

What he kept showed what he was: passports,
Wartime identity card, rare photographs
Snapped on his business travels or, much later on,
As a tired and portly district councillor.

He'd be leaving for work: polishing his shoes,
Checking his silk tie, kissing his wife goodbye;
A dewy garden carnation in his buttonhole,
His handkerchief folded to its alpine peak.

Or returning: *News* and *Standard* flung aside,
Reaching for the decanter, the evening's first sherry,
Smelling of the world and his smoky journey home –
The last steam train from London Bridge to Reigate.

Then he'd be away for days or weeks at a time,
Piecing together Europe's shattered glassware,
His passports crammed with kaleidoscopic visas;
The People's Republic of Yugoslavia takes a page.

It's Belgium and Holland mostly: his closest friends
The Wautys and the Dehandschutters of Manage,
And always, in Maastricht, the Mager Brothers
Who sounded, I thought, like something out of films.

And surely Willy Mager took these photographs,
In their continental treacle-tinted colour:
My father relaxed, ironic, in command,
Looking for once the statesman he should have been.

My mother's with him (I'm packed off at school),
More beautiful and happier than I remember her
On the emotional see-saw of our life at home.
It strikes me now that she's in love: with whom?

Unanswerable still. She stayed loyal to her man,
The father I've come too late to understand,
As I rummage through these remnants of identity:
His passports, a few photographs, and me.

The Lindshammar Pig

This glassblower's cheeks are bulbous as Dizzy Gillespie's
As he forms what must surely be a blue glass flask.
He'll add four feet, two ears, blob eyes, a curly tail,
And seal the aperture to create a stumpy snout.

But in truth he's ruined it: that slit along the back
Turns it into a piggy-bank, a glowing deep-blue toy.
'It would be great as a pig, without the slit,' says the boy.
'Okay' – and the glassblower smiles – 'for you I make one.'

We have come to Vetlanda, in the east of Sweden,
By slow train from cabbage-coloured Gothenburg,
Steaming in a warm wet summer. Some long hours later,
The pig is boxed and cotton-woolled, safe for its journey.

Caught in a North Sea storm, the ferry runs six hours late;
His mother brings the seasick boy a peach, then eats it.
Asked at Tilbury Customs, 'Anything to declare?'
The boy replies winningly: 'Yes, I have a blue pig.'

Now the Lindshammar pig surveys a Suffolk snowfield
And everybody from that day in Vetlanda is dead,
Except for the boy and, in a manner of speaking, the pig.
If there's an afterlife, the glassblower will be smiling.

Strand, 1923

No shadows here: the distance recedes in mist;
A London Particular's inching up the river.
Crowds fill the pavement and the open-topped buses;
One or two of them have read *The Waste Land*.

A poster: 'Break any engagement to see *Ambush*.'
Another suggests a trip to *Little Old New York*.
Handbag beneath her arm, clothes unshowy but good,
Mrs Dalloway passes the Strand Palace Hotel.

And no one has noticed the photographer –
Except, from the back of a horse-drawn covered wagon,
Propped among sacks and packages, the grocer's boy
Smiles shyly at the camera and the future.

Louis Takes a Break

Meanwhile, elsewhere: in Richmond, Indiana,
Seven musicians huddle round a horn
Which, like the Strand's unnoticed camera,
Records the moment. Yes, a star is born.

Because the second cornet's so majestic,
They've put him at the back where he won't drown
Honoré's trombone or Johnny's blackstick;
A wise move, that, until those chimes ring down.

Then something happens: Louis takes a break.
The hot news from America fills our ears:
A sound too proud and noble to mistake,
Across the wow and flutter of the years.

King Oliver's Creole Jazz Band: 'Chimes Blues' (7 April 1923)

JOHN MUCKLE

Out of Town

ROBERT DUNCAN, *The H.D. Book* (University of California Press) $49.95

MICHAEL MCCLURE, *Of Indigo and Saffron: New and Selected Poems* (University of California Press) $34.95

Harriet Tarlo (ed.), *The Ground Aslant: An Anthology of Radical Landscape Poetry* (Shearsman Books) £12.95

Robert Duncan's whole poetic journey began in a high school classroom when his teacher, Miss Keough, read him H.D.'s imagist poem 'Heat'. The dreamy boy, locked into the Eng. Lit. curriculum of a school designed to turn out well-balanced upper-middle-class machines to run corporate America, noticed that there was a special way Miss Keough spoke of, read aloud from or alluded to certain literary works, as though they formed a secret tradition, almost forbidden, unofficial, and certainly subversive in the extreme emotions and selfish vaulting hopes they engendered; but somehow, he intuited in her presence, these charged words were central to what reading, and to what was alive and dangerous in all culture, was all about. Miss Keough's favourites included Hardy, Lawrence, the Brontës, English Romantic poets, romantic American modernists, Amy Lowell, Joyce and Woolf and Pound – all of it leaping in radical implication out of this short poem of H.D.'s, which Duncan obsessively unpacks and returns to throughout *The H.D. Book*. Miss Keough seems to have served up this hidden tradition to her class in glimpses, flashing vistas, sparking in Duncan the idea that this high pure radical tradition was somehow feminine in its voice, its concerns, its basic tenor, and – a crucial word – had been *occulted*, deliberately hidden, and never allowed to shine properly. Also, it had something of the glamour of the occult, of forbidden liberatory knowledges and the erotically charged rituals devised to surround and propitiate them. H.D.'s poem was a conjuration of a desiring power, of an orgasmic release, and it begins to develop the rhythmic and narrative energy of her erotically charged classical sequences:

> O wind, rend open the heat,
> Cut apart the heat
> Rend it to tatters.
>
> Fruit cannot drop
> Through this thick air –
> Fruit cannot fall into heat
> That presses up and blunts
> The points of pears
> And rounds the grapes.
>
> Cut the heat –
> plough through it,
> turning it on either side
> of your path.
>
> (from 'Heat')

The H.D. Book is framed as a defence of what Duncan sees as a feminine poetic tradition, or at least one in which women's ways of thinking and writing are taken to be central, which is to say they are definitely central to his own understanding of the ongoing project of radical American poetry of the mid-century. It is therefore important in American poetry in a double sense, providing a complete – though never finished – map of a series of intellectual relationships between American modernist poetry and its successors and an unreconstructed, full-blown nineteenth-century Romanticism such as seems to have survived better in America than anywhere else, as well as radically revaluing the contribution of women (and, later, all non-dominant social groups) to what he sees as an ongoing culture of radical resistance to American capitalism; but it is H.D.'s fabulous travels and her Hellenism that birth him into the elaboration of a notion of the scope of 'Poetry' and 'the Poet' central to his vision of culture; a web he never quite finished spinning.

Duncan's method of composition in this poetic credo, which he worked on mainly from 1959 to 1964, was an unusual one, as his editors Michael Boughn and Victor Coleman point out in their excellent introduction. Beginning conventionally enough with scribbled notes, he gradually subsumed these into finished drafts which were again revised and added to, and … added to again, recast and refined, expanded and qualified, re-edited, and further beautified in a never-ending process which saw him through partial serial publication, an aborted book deal with a frustrated editor, and eventually to posthumous glory in this large meticulously edited volume of his critical masterpiece. They call his method 'accretive'. Robert Creeley once described Whitman's poetry as 'agglomerative', meaning that it grew, not moss, but by means of such things as might well stick to a rolling rock: mud and sticks, fresh broken foliage and all manner of small interesting items that happened to be in its path, and so *Leaves of Grass* grew proportionately with each new edition. The same might be said of *The H.D. Book*, for whereas in a lesser writer a sense of circularity and drift and slow accumulation might be maddening, Duncan's exquisite sensibility, his exploration of the early Pound of *The Spirit of Romance* and his strong grasp of his version of Romantic thought, really does amplify and enrich his readings of his subject, and in case we should miss a connection with Whitman, his lifelong partner Jess provides a frontispiece collage in which Duncan, Walt Whitman, Shakespeare, Socrates and a few other classical dudes are all brought together in a kind of Mount Rushmore group portrait of Great Minds for the Ages. But apart from a few small blemishes, this is a beautiful and fascinating book.

Michael McClure once told a story about showing a freshly published copy of *Bending the Bow* to Bob Dylan in a café. As McClure earnestly explained how long Duncan had worked on this book, that it was the outcome of intense poetic meditation, represented the partial fulfilment of a life's project and that the poet had vowed to abstain from publishing anything else for fifteen years, the Minnesotan marvel skimmed through it quickly, nodding his head, before rapidly returning the volume to his coffee-time companion – covered in large greasy thumbprints from a pastry he had been eating. He gave McClure an autoharp for a present. His place in the other chair at Robert Duncan's Thoreauvian retreat, and sitting right there bang opposite Dylan in a pricey Frisco sandwich bar, both say he deserved it; being in the right place at the right time to be a poet, so centred, as his poems are, in the present, savouring the impermanent moment of being.

This is a place he always seems to occupy and to write from, and perhaps explains the sense of suspension and sameness in all his poetry, from *Hymns to St Geryon* (1959) to *Plum Stones: Cartoons of No Heaven* (2002) and *Swirls in Asphalt* (2011). It is a place of 'contingent flux' where 'being' is apparently being fought for, or maybe just experienced in the moment, but nothing much really seems to happen despite all the news of revolutions and struggles and spiritual striving he tries to bring in. No drama. Nothing of anguish, of difficulty, of struggle. Nothing but self-awareness, self-presence and the feeling of relentless unpuncturable self-regard.

> THE MOMENT IS OUR
> real body
> as are all moments
> mutually arising
> together.
> Your eyes
> are moonrise.
> Each moment
> is the gate
> of emancipation.
> Swelling with pride
> I'm
> here
> with dark hair
> in a green Scottish
> jacket
> (from 'THE MOMENT IS OUR')

As this poem continues McClure falls back on narration, and on allegory, in order to tell us the whole violent story of natural existence: 'the eagle / flying over / with the dead / gazelle calf / in her claws / while the jackal / runs beneath her / jumping / and / barking'. But catharsis, history, and involvement are denied as even this horrific spectacle is undercut by his affectless upper-case shouting that 'THERE / ARE / NO / LESSONS'. It is a poetry of a consciousness in which everything is interconnected in the same plane, every moment and experience co-existent. But if each moment flows into and out of every other, equivalent, coterminous and finally indistinguishable, how can each be the gate of an emancipation? Perhaps none of them is, and we are left only with the repeated emptiness of this seemingly all-embracing perception, this nowness and its insight, until the acid finally wears off. McClure seems to float above his own work, his ideas, his creation, as these diamond-like 'cartoons of no heaven' continue to pop into his mind, still with great energy and clarity.

A number of the British poets gathered in Harriet Tarlo's anthology *The Ground Aslant* owe at least something to figures of the San Francisco Renaissance and to the special confluence of Romantic and modernist elements in their vision of a radical, transformative poetry. Not everyone is willing to see in Wordsworth's great crowd of golden daffodils the angrily nodding yellow bonnets of a host of radical democratic protestors, ready to uproot themselves and trail, triffid-like, across the English dales; but despite this embarrassment, and a more immediate connection to the British avant-garde, particularly to its connections with Olsonian projectivism, with its new kind of landscape and bottom-up history writing, its formal declaration that 'A foot is to kick with' and its assertion that new forms must be 'Equal, That Is, to the Real itself', many do connect strongly with *Lyrical Ballads*: its tilting vistas apprehended in a rush, its leech-gatherers, its 'peopled landscape', its ruins, its traces, its quality of being stark, elemental and dreamy. And like Duncan's, this book comes out of a female-inflected sense of Romanticism and modernism, with the work of Frances Presley, Helen MacDonald, Wendy Mulford, Elizabeth Bletsoe, Carol Watts, Zoë Skoulding and Tarlo herself rightly given equal time with a fascinating group of well-excavated male poets, making this a book of feminised landscapes, intensely botanised, delicate but strongly observant, adventurous, aiming, as Coleridge praised Dorothy Wordsworth, to be 'a perfect electro-meter' of the rural pulse.

Elisabeth Bletsoe is a good place to start: a witchly interest in herbs, psychology, an open-field poetics mapping dreamscapes, birds in flight, scenes of the hare hunt; an exquisite lore-filled vocabulary, an air of dark ritual and occulted knowledge – all of which Robert Duncan would have greatly admired. She is a rivetingly violent writer:

> I torce the necks of wounded gamebirds,
> shock of come-apart cervicals, reflex
>   wingjumps, (feeling
> a pulse not my heart,
> the once-complete potential in
> soft declensions of egg-buds
>
> unspathing the spadix of
> wild arum   to bare
> male-&-female in one bulb:
> a scent of putrefaction &
> warm hairiness
> drawing flies across the meniscus
>   (from 'Cross-in-Hand')

Her poetry takes pleasure in language itself, in lexical items like 'unspathing' and 'spadex' and 'egg-buds', the mysterious spell and astmosphere of flower-names in their own right, quite separate from the prolific and unmemorable weeds they both denote and elevate into poetry. It is these elements in most of the poets herein (women and men), simultaneous involvement with and removal from the environments they write of, and an overriding interest in making small pretty objects out of words, which connect them back to the Imagist tradition, and, if Duncan is right, to a deeply feminine strain in modernist poetry.

This anthology's version of pastoral is 'a peopled landscape' but peopled with what? Pope's 'myriads in the peopled grass' are largely absent; there are a few faint echoes of John Clare's magnificent insect courts or tiny pregnant mice, his closeness, weirdness, estrangement; but a poet like Colin Simms seems to plug straight into the main artery of Romantic nature poetry with his obsessive recoveries of witnessed moments of interaction with otters and martens: this is about observation, an experience of being there, and achieves a near-mystical communion with the momentariness and intermittence of the observed world; his long, impacted lines seem to be lying in wait, stalking the immediate perceptual world for glimpses, hidden movements, revelations of a small alien life in the undergrowth. These are his spots in time, moments of revivifying virtue. In his semi-mythological poem 'Carcajou' he becomes an Indian tracker in the American wilderness, so fused with the life of his quarry that he often changes places with the giant ancestral marten of his imagination, a seed of descended life, a non-human Adam of the wild places, because, for Simms, we are all members of the weasel family.

What might be called his 'inhumanism' reminds me of another Californian poet, Robinson Jeffers, for whom the animal and natural world with all its innate violence and cyclical generating processes have an absolute primacy and centrality, human presence at best that of a deluded interloper, more usually contemptible, vain, destructive. Simms is a more modest writer, aware of his frailty before the natural world and activities that have consumed him, an agreeably human-scale witness:

> second-generation mechanician I am   not the indigene
> that from the beginning was like this, adaptable   the
> so-called   Indian
> whose trail we all must find   I sit a metal rid-rind
> rust and laugh (you've seen the oxidised stripe on
> my side!)
> laugh-grind
> (from 'Carcajou')

Jaques, one of the exiled courtiers in the Forest of Arden in Shakespeare's *As You Like It*, claims that 'I can suck melancholy out of a song as a weasel sucks eggs', and whilst he is mocked for an indulgent fop who spends all day tearfully watching water from a stream drip into the crying dying eyes of a wounded stag, he is also able to 'moralise the spectacle' for the amusement of the banished Duke as the 'fat and greasy citizens' of the herd pass by their fallen 'bankrupt':

> Thus most invectively he pierceth through
> The body of the city, country, court,
> Yea, and this our life; swearing that we
> Are mere usurpers, tyrants, and what's worse
> To fright the animals and kill them up
> In their assigned and native dwelling place.
> (from *As You Like It*, Act II Sc. 1)

Is this the beginning of eco-poetry? Of Romantic social criticism derived from the observation of nature? Of a wholesale importation of human politics into the mapping of a largely non-human environment? Peter Riley's lifelong exploration of what a post-Romantic pastoral poetry might look like shows him to be well aware that if the retreats of rambler, hill-walker and communer with the elements in out-of-the-way places are, like the Forest of Arden, apparently places in which to hide from the complexities and betrayals of court-life, they almost always lead out onto perilous ledges where its politics prove inescapable. We rediscover life's real problems everywhere, as in practically every poem by this beautiful poet, who is able to will the landscapes he inhabits to speak in tongues:

> I walk back to Beresford in the afternoon.
> The coal tit, dyed in modern philosophy,
> flits for nuts. Snow on the shoulder, sky
> narrowed between hill and hill a blue-grey
> tongue for any speech is distant at the time.
> Silence lines the horizon, glowing to a lost
> nation, snow-brushed fields glossing the vein
> to a hole in tense, a history of light
> or moving pain to paper an agreement is touched,
> that death shall have no choice.
> (from 'Alstonefield')

The Scottish poet Thomas A. Clark is represented here by a single sequence, 'The Grey Fold', of miniatures, which takes one of the formal ambitions of this kind of poetry – to find an effortless line that is as clear as an uncluttered prospect – to its most refined point (unless to place words engraved on stone within a landscape, like Ian Hamilton Finlay) in poems that are formed into tiny perfect meditative maps of moments of landscape and inscape:

> an astonishment
> prolonged
> as if it were raining
> stillness
> (from 'The Grey Fold')

Ian Davidson from North Wales is amongst the most directly political of these writers; the way he often notices faint animal tracks, half-hidden traces, recalls Peter Riley, but he aspires to Clark's cleanness and his quality of disclosure, attempting to achieve immediacy of perception by means of breathless run-ons and crammed parataxis. He finds the Taliban lurking in caves on Anglesey, along with Owen Glendower, and asks: 'what commentary / might a broadsword receive how / deep can a covering be'; under their clean surfaces his poems are busy with thought, and anxieties, as though his deepest beliefs of self and region are forever besieged on all sides by political and career paranoias, by 'real life':

> he saw himself pretending to
> doubt and that was enough
> the queue outside the town hall
> spread down the street the projector
> was useless with that size of crowd
> (from 'Human Remains & Sudden Movements')

Tony Baker's object-modernism, highly wrought out of short, darting journeys; Peter Larkin's occluded landscapes; Nicholas Johnson's careering progresses; Mark Goodwin's broken and gapped words, and Mark Dickinson's intimate and musical sea-side lyrics, all are equally deserving of this reviewer's airtime. But for now I'd like to return to Robert Duncan's and perhaps Tarlo's idea that there is an especially feminine locus in modernism – and, by extension, in this kind of Romantic-modernist radical landscape writing.

Helen Macdonald is a fine example, a good poet of the Cambridge school whose choppy headlong personal meditations reminded me of Denise Riley, a little, and who alludes to Douglas Oliver's phrase 'inside the harm is a clearing' (not such a good place for a picnic, maybe) and has something of the feeling of his early poems, such as 'When I Was First at Bridport', in 'Walking':

Where. Why and etcetera. The head bows and nothing is.
Shielding the harm from further harm is harder than this.
Voile & velux and little owls calling through dawn
mate selection, early spring on ash fence, white dots
a clave dancing sweetly on the posts. Not a call to arms
but I'm shaking anyway, and the sweet dawn is when
the wind gets up, half past four, cold on my face in the
    barn
in the sense of a resister only: still alive, still hurt, whatever.
    (from 'Walking')

Macdonald's poetry weeps and stumbles over many a miry slough, rambles across wind-swept crags, and, gazing out to sea, looks again for the pitching of birds ('Who cares if it flies again / flying things / dumb objects which flinch and fall again') with the eye of a restless, anguished observer who is untaken in by the 'idiocy of quietude', swerving in mid-flight, coming to, coming back to herself as a poised consciousness, an acute language-user whose vocabulary isn't too countrified after all, dips into French, and, like the poetry of Riley, D., turns out to be reflecting wryly on itself, or like that of O'Hara, F., on why it is not a painter – in her case a love of movement, intellectual speculation and shifting vantage points. Is this what O'Hara meant by 'blonde, feminine and tough'?

Wendy Mulford is a pioneer of Cambridge feminist poetry, her work here more an affair of steady tramping, historical noticing and judicious flower identification than wildly calling out for Heathcliff, although the Suffolk countryside is always a place to remember what you have lost, take stock, and consider small frail boats bobbing at anchor in the mouth of the Deben:

divinity, what is
heaven is it haven
to lose the harbour is one night's work
or slower
tempests take up a
lifetime's tacking to lie
in calm water all currents devious deep
driving or
air upstead currents breathing, insteps spread to
sun's balm
dream the poisoned source
renew
    (from 'A Tale of Loss')

Carol Watts writes strongly from within a sense of the countryside as a working environment, in touch with the economics of husbandry, its quotas, subsidies, and the perils of sheep-farming as bureaucratised agro-business; her 'Zeta Landscape' has a built-in critique of Romantic pastoral's 'climbing to infinity' as a recreational/spiritual experience, and instead asks prosaic, practical questions in order to uncover 'the truth of this place':

do these add up are they outside subsidy or
logged in magnitudes of adjustment the value
of a warm animal less then the cost of quantifying
its warmth or inspecting animation each sixteen
days the collisions of neighbouring hillsides result
today in corpses by the river seven blown fleeces
    (from 'Zeta Landscape')

Perhaps if this is all there was to her sequence of expanded sonnets, they might grow dull, but there is also an air of precision, a quickness of involvement, a fierce protective spikiness in them, which keeps you reading on and on: she really does like sheep.

Zoë Skoulding has some very elegant, well-composed love poems, about walking in forests and saying goodbye, which fuse longing with a liking for ideas, they're lovely; and some others which resemble slender tree trunks. Harriet Tarlo likes to spread out, use the page, accost people and see what they have to say about collecting scrap. Frances Presley's poetry is immersed in the childhood places of her girlhood in Somerset, well-worked memories still yielding bright tin. Robert Duncan was much exercised by the idea of female silliness: male critics who had accused H.D. of silliness for her mystical high seriousness damaged her reputation and propelled his passionate defence of her. He wanted to reclaim the silly, the seemingly trivial, the outlandish mystical belief, rapture and sensitivity, perhaps even feyness, as being at the core of what he valued in feminine sensibility and thought. Delicacy and refinement and precise arrangement are certainly qualities that Presley, and others, exhibit here. An idea that it's perfectly okay to do something small, that might be cut into a stone.

patched patchouli
absterrent hardering

made hepworth
veiled but more expressive
than a gormley

look there's a small orange
    (from 'West Anstey longstone')

Whether or not Harriet Tarlo and her contributors share Robert Duncan's occult Romanticism, or his exalted – and gay – take on the feminine, or H.D.'s erotics and 'hermetic definitions', they are to be warmly congratulated for continuing with this kind of writing about rural life and its changing place in the cultural economies of signs and space of this century. Pastoral may be long ago and far away. But now it's night-time in the big city. Half-understanding, I zip up my windcheater and slip out onto the empty streets of Harringay, to buy milk and cigarettes from the all-night garage.

PIER PAOLO PASOLINI

Poems Around Town

Translated from the Italian by N.S. Thompson

April 23, 1962

A carpet of primroses. Sheep
against the light (yes, put on
the 50mm, Tonino, don't worry
if there's too much light – let's do
this shot against nature!).
Grass on the Acqua Santa, cold and warm,
yellow and soft, old and new.
Sheep and shepherd, a fragment
of Masaccio (try the 75mm
and a dolly move to close up).
Medieval spring. A heretic Saint
(called 'Blasphemy' by his cronies.
He'll be a pimp, as usual. Ask
doleful Leonetti for advice
on medieval prostitution).
Then action. A working-class passion
(endless tracking shot with Mary
moving forward, asking after her son
in Umbrian dialect, singing her agony in Umbrian).
Spring brings a carpet
of hard young grass, soft young grass, primroses…
and an atrophy of the senses mixed with lust.
After the visionary shot (impious graveyard
romps of tarts),
a 'prayer' in the blazing fields.
Tarts, pimps, thieves, peasants,
hands clasped under their faces
(all with the 50mm against the light).
I'll film the sunniest Apennines.
When the 60s are as forgotten
as the eleventh century
and my skeleton hasn't even
any nostalgia for the world,
what will my 'private life' matter then,
miserable skeletons without even a private
or public life? Blackmailers!
What will matter then? Only my tenderness will matter
in the spring after death
and I'll win the bet in the fury
of my love for Acqua Santa in the sun.

April 23, 1962

Skeletons in Toscano suit,
a Battistoni tie (in millions, Easter Monday
holiday's enough to give an idea of them).
Immense convex fields in panorama
show groups worthy of Mizoguchi
(fresh grass – grown out of the hellish,
intoxicating April light, light
for reeking shepherds – below,
a universal backdrop: *grisaille* survivors
in the foreground, berets green
above brick- or cherry-red jackets,
gleaming family cars, picturesque
groups playing with a ball,
a *déjeuner sur l'herbe* at ease,
with curtains or rugs out in the sun:
in the background, the precise outline
of eastern outskirts: whitewash and bricks
on roofless square Capernaums
spread out over the outline
of immense convex fields
where millions of living skeletons are grazing).
Moravia consoles me about their plans:
they wouldn't want me killed off
by the cancer of scandal, because then
I'd belong to the ruling class.
(..
..........[omitted]) Ah, yes, the bourgeoisie
means hypocrisy, but also
hate. Hate wants a victim
and that victim is one man. The light's monumental,
quick, quick, let's make use of it, quick,
the 50mm and the dolly moving in front:
Mamma Roma and her son are walking
to the new house among radiating
housing blocks there, where the sun spreads its archaic
wings: if the light gives way,
turn these moving bodies into wooden
statues, faded Masaccio figures
with bright white cheeks and opaque
black rings around the eyes – those
of the time of primroses, cherries
and the first barbarian invasions in
the 'burning rays of ancient Italian suns'…
These stage-set Ina-Casa blocks are altars
retreating in the Bullicante Light
to Cecafumo. Altars of working-class
glory. I think in peace about
my skeleton, my dust, in the millennia:
and painfully about the living
skeletons of the bourgeoisie on the look-out
for evil – in truth, Possession,
as a pretext, Sex – there where death's
more impartial in the dissolving shot.

April 25, 1962

When a troupe invades
tonight's streets, it'll be a new era.
Therefore have fun with this sorrow, too.

The idea of making a film about your suicide
thunders through the millennia... going back
to Shakespeare... It's sex, the grandeur
of the libido, its sweetness...
The protagonist is butchered:
a bubble of air inflates his skin,
he's so terrified he could fly.
A cleft splits him from palate
to breastbone and sends tremors
throughout his body: the poisoning
perforates his stomach, gives him diarrhoea.
Suicide's the simplest idea
that can come to him: meanwhile, he enters
a cinema (it's years since he's done it,
like this, alone) and above the brief surface
of his visceral pangs, there
in alternating montage, the huge
colourful surface of the commercials.
Refrigerators, toothpastes, smiling
cheeks. Then out he goes.
Night, with the scent of lime trees,
although it's late April, nearly May.
But that year, spring was late
in getting started. The city was gleaming bright,
headlights quivering in that glow
of easy effect – damp, heavy,
heavier than the smell of the compressed lime trees
spreading in the air –
headlights of trams and cars quivering
in silent orgasm
as if in atomic flight to the world's
last or its latest supper:
masses of churning lights,
beaming along the curving ring road.
In illogical sequence, you then see
him walking in the even more remote
outskirts: hedges dripping,
walls of old farms... and a sudden quiet
space, almost springlike, with the moon perhaps
above low-knit clouds:
in the middle of that sweet-smelling space,
that emptiness of rural freedom,
you can hear dogs barking and the festive
voices of children – those of the eleventh century
or of a future far off. A distant pistol
shot. And 'The End'. Oh,
hedges dripping, slope swelling
with shameless springtime grass
on hills pierced by quarries,
sweet Thebaids where Nature, ignored
by the new men, is celebrating April.

May 13, 1962

I watch the troupe idling about in an overcast
hour of rain and note how – in the confusion
that makes everyone equal, forms
that have no doubts about being human
or the way they have human faces
and desires – each one of them
knows how to look
self-satisfied. Narcissism,
the only consoling force, the only salvation!
On every level, from the extra
(because she's close to the head of the group) to
the director (because he's aware of the art),
no one lacks the instinct for self-affirmation,
precisely because they are what they are.
One leans against a wall, dark as he is,
as he has to be; one laughs,
legs apart in a doorway,
laughing because in irony
every illicit desire seems better overcome;
one's silent there, sitting on a crate,
but even someone silent
has his troubles to give him satisfaction;
one's content with a cruel young face,
another with the equally
cruel face of an old slum dweller;
one hints at his solid friendships,
provided they mean a single step up;
one with a Spanish look
– a Caravaggio – puffs himself up with the work,
and another one, work-shy – a Gemito –
with idleness. The most illiterate working class
and the most ignorant bourgeoisie in Europe.
Gianduia, look through the pan glass
to see if the sun could come back; I watch
the clouds breaking up over the rooftops
of the six-storey altars of Cecafumo
spread symmetrically over
the Caetani's dark fields. Only the sun
imprinting film can express
a touch of age-old love in so much age-old hate.

June 10, 1962

A lone ruin, dream of an arch,
of Roman or Romanesque vaulting,
in a field foaming with sunlight
whose heat is as calm as a sea:
crumbling there the ruin is unloved.
Usage and liturgy now profoundly extinct
live on in its style – and in the sun –
for those who understand its presence and poetry.
Take a few steps and you're on the Appia
or the Tuscolana: where everything is life
for everyone. Or rather, those who know
nothing of style and history are accessory
to that life, whose meanings become confused
in sordid stillness, indifference
and violence. Thousands,
thousands of people, buffoons
of a fiery modernity, in the sun
whose meaning is also in action,
pass each other on the streets,
swarming darkly over the blinding pavements
against the Ina-Casa blocks lost in the sky.
I am a force of the Past.
My love is only in tradition.
I come from the ruins, the churches,
the altarpieces, from villages abandoned

in the Apennines or Alpine foothills,
where brethren used to live.
I wheel about the Tuscolana like a madman,
on the Appia like a dog without its master.
Or I gaze at the dusks, the mornings over
Rome, over the world, like the first acts of Post-History,
which I witness by right of residence
from the far edge of some buried
age. Whoever is born from the viscera
of a dead woman is monstrous.
And I, adult foetus, wander about,
more modern than modern,
searching for brethren who no longer exist.

June 12, 1962

We see ourselves in projection
and here's the city naked in a miserable hour,
terrifying like all nakedness.
A burnt-out landscape whose flames
were extinguished this afternoon or in the millennia,
an unending circle of pinkish ruins,
charred wood and bleaching bones, rain-washed
scaffolding, burnt by fresh sun.
The radiant Appia swarms with thousands
of insects – today's men – the Neorealist
obsessives of today's vernacular Chronicles.
Then Testaccio appears in that honeyed light
projected onto earth from beyond the tomb.
Perhaps the Bomb's been dropped
without my realising it. In fact, there's no doubt about it.
And the End of the World's already come,
a mute thing, dropped in the twilight shadow.
Whoever's involved in this age is a Shade.
Oh, holy Twentieth Century, region of the soul
in which the Apocalypse is only a past event!
Pontormo with a meticulous cameraman
has arranged corners of yellowish houses
to cut this soft friable light
which, from the yellow sky, turns a golden-dusted
brown on the world of city dwellers...
And like plants without roots, houses and men
create only silent monuments of light and shade
in motion: because their death is in movement.
They go as if without any soundtrack,
cars and lorries under the arches
on the asphalt by the gasometer
in a golden hour like that of Hiroshima
twenty years on, always deeper into
that gesticulating death of theirs: and
late for death, too early for the true life,
I drink the incubus of light like a glittering wine.
Nation without hopes! The Apocalypse
exploded beyond their awareness
in the sadness of a Mannerist Italy
has killed everyone: look at them, shades
dripping gold in the golden throes of death.

June 21, 1962

I work all day like a monk
and wander through the night like an alley cat
looking for love... I should offer myself
for sainthood to the Curia.
In fact, I reply to mystification
with meekness. As if through a camera
I see the posse at the lynching,
watch myself massacred with the calm
courage of a scientist. I seem
to feel hate and instead write
verses full of meticulous love.
I study treachery as if it were inevitable,
as if I weren't its object.
Yet I feel pity for the Fascists, young
and old, whom I consider forms
of the most vicious evil.
I oppose only the violence of reason.
I am passive as a bird in flight
which sees everything
but as it skims through the sky
carries in its heart
a conscience that does not forgive.

Notes

This diary sequence was written in 1962 while filming *Mamma Roma*, Pasolini's second feature film, about an ex-prostitute and her son attempting a new respectable life in the Roman suburbs. Lines from *June 10, 1962* (ll. 22–39) were used in the short film *La ricotta* (1962) about filming a religious epic and spoken by the director (played by Orson Welles, dubbed by Giorgio Bassani), which formed part of the collective feature *RoGoPaG* (1963), with contributions by Rosellini, Godard, Pasolini and Gregoretti.

Tonino delli Colli: director of photography on *Mamma Roma*.
Acqua Santa: ruins around a famous spring south of Rome, encroached on by housing developments in the 50s and 60s.
Masaccio (1401–28): Florentine painter of the early Renaissance.
Leonetti, Francesco (b. 1924): poet and novelist.
Mizoguchi, Kenji (1898–1956): Japanese film director.
Moravia, Alberto (1907–90): novelist and critic.
Ina-Casa: medium-rise housing built by the Istituto Nazionale Assicurazione (National Insurance Institute).
Cecafumo: Roman district.
Caravaggio (1573–1610): Neapolitan painter of the early Baroque.
Gemito, Vincenzo (1852–1929): Neapolitan sculptor.
Gianduia: production assistant.
Caetani: Roman ducal landowning family.
Appia, Tuscolana: highways south out of Rome.
Ciociaria: rural region south of Rome.
Chronicles: contemporary histories of the thirteenth and fourteenth centuries.
Testaccio: working-class quarter of Rome.
Pontormo (1494–1557): Florentine Mannerist painter.

IAN BRINTON

Jack Spicer's Words: 'God Must Have a Big Eye'

In the issue of *Archeus* (1989) devoted to the work of Andrew Crozier, Geoffrey Ward wrote about the unpunctual nature of language:

> Language is doomed to unpunctuality, words chasing, describing, shadowing a reality they can do anything but actually *be*. But if words miss their goal they pursue in the meantime their own life in the mouth or on the page, powerful figures of speech that predate our individual use of them, constraining or permitting meanings always aslant or surplus to requirements.

With an Orphic sense of inevitability our words can only record our loss, acting as totemic symbols of what is already ghost. The third poem in the sequence of Crozier's 'The Veil Poem' opens with the lines

> In nature everything, we suppose, connects up
> with everything else...

Ward suggested that the inclusion of the word 'suppose' cuts off access to the connection 'except in moments of expanded awareness that give Crozier's poetry both its tacit pathos and its fixture within the rhetorics of Romanticism'. Crozier's full awareness of the distance of language in its yearning for connectedness is intriguingly brought out when one looks at the earliest draft of those lines from 'The Veil Poem'. In a manuscript titled 'The first five sections of SEVEN VEILS OF WISDOM IN TEN CARDS a return for Jeff Morsman' Crozier's opening line to section three runs:

> In nature everything, we suppose, is connected
> with everything else...

The manuscript is dated 7 January 1972 and has the amendment 'connects up' inserted in pencil at the top of the page. The first publication of the poem came soon after in *Sesheta* (Spring 1972). The original wording 'is connected' has a flat sense of information about it, whereas the change to 'connects up' conveys, in its present tense, a quality of movement that makes the intervention of the phrase 'we suppose' even more effective as a record of reflective distance between the word and the action. In *PN Review* 192 (March–April 2010) Geoffrey Ward returned to his theme in an article about 'Poetry and the Rift', taking a quotation from Jack Spicer as his title, 'I announce the death of Orpheus':

> In the beginning was the word. Trouble being, the word was always late for the event.
>
> Words can describe, evoke, suggest, delineate, propose, haunt – do all manner of things – except *be* the thing or feeling or concept to which they refer. The verbal sign, while conjuring in the ear or on the page a simulacrum, (perhaps a beautiful, a crafted and convincing replicant, but a simulacrum nonetheless) can never be other than: a word. This is not a problem in everyday transactions, and indeed our development of language is possibly our greatest and our defining achievement. We certainly handle words better than we handle each other or the non-human world. But living in particular spaces, whereby the hieroglyphs that spell 'save the planet' are not the same thing as a saved planet, the injunction 'pass the salt' no guarantee of approaching salinity, there is, built into writing, a certain lateness. There is something of death in all its usages.

Those 'rhetorics of Romanticism' can be accessed of course by any close study of the poetry and letters of John Keats. For instance, in April 1819, at around the time he was composing the 'Ode on a Grecian Urn', Keats wrote to George and Georgiana Keats about a dream he had recently had and how the attempt to use the words of poetry to recapture it was doomed to failure:

> The fifth canto of Dante pleases me more and more – it is that one in which he meets with Paolo and Francesca – I had passed many days in rather a low state of mind and in the midst of them I dreamt of being in that region of Hell. The dream was one of the most delightful enjoyments I ever had in my life – I floated about the whirling atmosphere as it is described with a beautiful figure to whose lips mine were joined as it seemed for an age – and in the midst of all this cold and darkness I was warm – even flowery tree tops sprung up and we rested on them sometimes with the lightness of a cloud till the wind blew us away again – I tried a Sonnet upon it – there are fourteen lines but nothing of what I felt in it – O that I could dream it every night.[1]

That gap between the fluidity of life and the stillness of the word is drawn in a seemingly timeless fashion upon the surface of an urn where the 'fair youth' stands beneath trees that will never be bare, but the word's approximation to life is seen by Keats as a 'Cold Pastoral': finally Life has a warmth and mutability that contrasts with the echoes of a gone world held within the structures of Art.

The 'Imaginary Elegies, I–IV' were read by Jack Spicer at a San Francisco poetry conference sponsored by the Poetry Center, run by Ruth Witt-Diamant, in April 1957. The Boston poet John Wieners had already asked if he could publish these poems in the first issue of his forthcoming magazine, *Measure*. As Lewis Ellingham and Kevin Killian make clear in their admirable book on Spicer and the San Francisco Renaissance, *Poet Be Like God*, Spicer regarded this suite of poems he had written for Robin Blaser as 'his best so far – and far too good for the upstart, know-nothing Wieners, who "only understands Black Mountain poetry and Cole Porter", neither of which Jack liked'. The reading was well attended and Robert Duncan produced some introductory notes which set the scene in a manner that must have been both intriguing and provocative:

> In his own work, Spicer disturbs. That he continues to do so is his vitality. The abortive, the solitary, the blasphemous, when they are not facetious, produce upheavals in the real. Life throws up the disturbing demand 'All is not well' – sign after sign generated of accusation manifest – which it is the daring of Spicer at times in poems to mimic. If you do not allow that life vomits; that the cosmos with its swollen and shrunken stars, its irruptions, vomits – you can refuse to allow only by denying fact.[2]

The opening of the first poem is startling in its clarity:

> Poetry, almost blind like a camera
> Is alive in sight only for a second. Click,
> Snap goes the eyelid of the eye before movement
> Almost as the word happens.
> One would not choose to blink and go blind
> After the instant. One would not choose
> To see the continuous Platonic pattern of birds flying
> Long after the stream of birds had dropped or had nested.
> Lucky for us that there are visible things like oceans
> Which are always around,
> Continuous, disciplined adjuncts
> To the moment of sight.
> Sight
> But not so sweet
> As we have seen.
> When I praise the sun or any bronze god derived from it
> Don't think I wouldn't rather praise the very tall blond boy
> Who ate all of my potato-chips at the Red Lizard.
> It's just that I won't see him when I open my eyes
> And I will see the sun.
> Things like the sun are always there when the eyes are open
> Insistent as breath.
>   One can only worship
> These cold eternals for their support of
> What is absolutely temporary.
> But not so sweet.
> The temporary tempts poetry
> Tempts photographs, tempts eyes.[3]

A camera freezes one moment in time and with that 'click' followed by a 'Snap' the moment is both caught and broken and, in a sense, the poem does become that 'continuous Platonic pattern of birds flying' which can be looked at, still life, by other people in other times. There is a slightly warmer tone to Spicer's awareness of life's movement than occurs in Keats's ode, where the phrase 'Cold Pastoral' distances the reader from the imagined world. Spicer's birds seem to hint at a more drawn-out movement still as they 'dropped and nested'.

Spicer is thankful for constant movement as opposed to stillness and the visible things, 'like oceans', draw him by being 'always around', their movement being continuous. There is an echo here perhaps of Hart Crane's yearning for beauty and annihilation in the second section of the sequence 'Voyages':

> Mark how her turning shoulders wind the hours,
> And hasten while her penniless rich palms
> Pass superscription of bent foam and wave, –
> Hasten, while they are true, – sleep, death, desire,
> Close round one instant in one floating flower.

This threat of the annihilation of the self is felt and analysed by the French phenomenologist, Francis Ponge, when he attempts a contemplation of any large, amorphous, monotonous or elemental mass such as the sea. With a humorous sense of rational distance he opens up his prose poem 'Bords de mer' ('Seashores'), from *Le Parti pris des choses*:

> La mer jusqu'à l'approche de ses limites est une chose simple qui se répète flot par flot. Mais les choses les plus simples dans la nature ne s'abordent pas sans y mettre beaucoups de formes, faire beaucoup de façons, les choses les plus épaisses sans subir quelque ameunisement. C'est pourquoi l'homme, et par rancune aussi contre leur immensité qui l'assomme, se précipite aux bords ou à l'intersection des grandes choses pour les définir. Car la raison au sein de l'uniforme dangereusement ballotte et se raréfie: un esprit en mal de notions doit d'abord s'approvisionner d'apparences.[4]

> [The sea right up to its very edges is a simple thing which repeats itself wave by wave. But the simplest things in Nature don't reach land without rather formal approaches, the putting on of airs and graces, where the thickest of things start to thin out. This is why man, begrudging of the immensity which stuns him, aims for the edges, the overlapping of things which provide them with definition. For Reason, tossed about within the bosom of the Uniform, becomes scarce: the mind seeking mental footholds needs to stock up on appearances.]

The camera of course offers precisely that 'edge', the separating of one moment from another within the stream and, by holding in front of us the picture of that which is irremediably gone, offers us the Orphic sense of the impossibility of return. The world of appearances, Art, consists of edges, contrasts, the meeting-points of different phenomena: individuality. It also acts as a constant reminder of what it is not. As Spicer puts it, the only reason for worshipping 'These cold eternals' is because of their 'support of / What is absolutely temporary'. And, of course, this freeze-frame world is 'not so sweet', but if we don't have God's 'big eye' then it is what we must reconcile ourselves to putting up with!

In his lecture on 'The Serial Poem and The Holy Grail', given in Vancouver on 15 June 1965, Spicer addressed this issue in terms of the difference between individual poems and the chronological world of a serial poem:

> A serial poem, in the first place, has the book as its unit – as an individual poem…has a poem as its unit, the actual poem that you write at the actual time, the single poem.[5]

A serial poem has to be chronological and it has to be 'where you just say, well, I'm going into the woods on a path that I have no idea about':

I'm not going to look backwards on the path at all or make Indian signs on the trees to see where I am… Not looking backwards. Letting the poem look forward. Just following the bloody path to see where it goes. And sometimes it doesn't go anywhere.

There is a sense here of the automatic poem and of a Dadaist movement at random. However, it is interesting to note that in the same lecture he returns to the freeze-frame imagery of 'Imaginary Elegies' when he refers to Robin Blaser's comments about serial poems:

Robin once said, in talking about a serial poem, that it's as if you go into a room, a dark room. A light is turned on for a minute. Then it's turned off again and you go into a different room where a light is turned on and turned off.

In one of the letters to the dead Spanish poet, Lorca, which Spicer incorporates into his serial poem 'After Lorca' he suggests teasingly how he wants poetry and the real world to combine:

I would like to make poems out of real objects. The lemon to be a lemon that the reader could cut or squeeze or taste – a real lemon like a newspaper in a collage is a real newspaper. I would like the moon in my poems to be a real moon, one which could be suddenly covered with a cloud that has nothing to do with the poem – a moon utterly independent of images. The imagination pictures the real. I would like to point to the real, disclose it, to make a poem that has no sound in it but the pointing of a finger.[6]

The temporary quality of a poem of that sort (read it before it decays on you and becomes something else!) may go some way to account for Spicer's air of indifference about the details of his publications. However, the idea of this collage decaying is something of which the poet takes full account:

But things decay, reason argues. Real things become garbage. The piece of lemon you shellac to the canvas begins to develop a mold, the newspaper tells of incredibly ancient events in forgotten slang, the boy becomes a grandfather. Yes, but the garbage of the real still reaches out into the current world making its objects, in turn, visible – lemon calls to lemon, newspaper to newspaper, boy to boy. As things decay they bring their equivalents into being.

There is something so settled about Keats's 'Ode on a Grecian Urn' and the poet's own awareness of how, when dealing with what is imitation of movement, his fixed vocabulary echoes beyond its mournful cadences, teases us readers 'out of thought':

Who are these coming to the sacrifice?
    To what green altar, O mysterious priest,
Lead'st thou that heifer lowing at the skies,
    And all her silken flanks with garlands drest?
What little town by river or sea shore,
    Or mountain-built with peaceful citadel,
        Is emptied of this folk, this pious morn?
And, little town, thy streets for evermore
Will silent be; and not a soul to tell
    Why thou art desolate, can e'er return.

Another of Spicer's letters to Lorca wrestles with this gap between immediacy and the stillness of what becomes transfixed into art:

It is very difficult. We want to transfer the immediate object, the immediate emotion to the poem – and yet the immediate always has hundreds of its own words clinging to it, short-lived and tenacious as barnacles. And it is wrong to scrape them off and substitute others. A poet is a time mechanic not an embalmer. The words around the immediate shrivel and decay like flesh around the body. No mummy-sheet of tradition can be used to stop the process. Objects, words must be led across time not preserved against it.

It was during the composition of 'After Lorca' that Spicer became aware of what he was involved with in terms of poetry and movement, and he wrote to Robin Blaser: 'Halfway through After Lorca I discovered that I was writing a book instead of a series of poems'. The letter, included in *Admonitions* (1957), goes on to describe Spicer's new aesthetic of the serial poem. As described by Ellingham and Killian, Spicer realised that his previous efforts at stand-alone poems had been futile and the search for the perfect poem had been meaningless. The letter continues:

Poems should echo and re-echo against each other. They should create resonances. They cannot live alone any more than we can… Things fit together. We knew that – it is the principle of magic. Two inconsequential things can combine together to become a consequence. This is true of poems too. A poem is never to be judged by itself alone. A poem is never by itself alone.

In the Vancouver lecture Spicer talked about the sense of time in the composition of a serial poem and pointed out that 'the book, which is a unit like a poem is, has to be absolutely chronological. It has to be chronological in the writing of the poems.' Using this idea he pointed to some interesting differences between his ideas of the serial poem and the great enterprises of Pound, Williams and Olson during the twentieth century:

Now this is the other thing that the serial poem is not, and Olson and Pound are good examples of that, although with both of them, the planned poem, the non-serial poem, can, if you get caught up in it, become a serial poem. Pound thought that the *Cantos* would end at Canto 100. He had said it many times to many college professors and really believed it. It had something to do with Dante. He was very, very unhappy and surprised, I'm sure, when there was Canto 101, 102, and so forth.
    With Charles Olson, the same thing happened with *The Maximus Poems*. He had an idea of what *The Maximus Poems* were when he started writing, and it changed as he's been going on. There will probably be Maximus poems for a long time. Now this is a kind of dictation that is a little bit different from the kind of dictation I was talking about last week. Of course, it's

dictation of form, you realize. It's not the same thing as dictation of lines, but it follows more or less the same laws. Olson started out with the idea, I guess, of a man facing human history and facing it from his own direction, which was Gloucester. The poems have gone by accretion to something more than that and I'm sure have scared him many times by the way they go.

At Robert Duncan's instigation Spicer sent the 'Imaginary Elegies' to *Poetry Chicago*, where they received a polite refusal; the first four of what eventually became a sequence of six were first published in Donald Allen's ground-breaking anthology from Grove Press in 1960, *The New American Poetry*. In a review of that book for the *New York Herald Tribune* Marianne Moore highlighted especially Spicer's

> firefly flash of insight, lightening with dry detachment, as here:

>> Poetry, almost blind like a camera
>> Is alive in sight only for a second. Click,

> the accents suiting the sense.

Although Spicer remained both fond and respectful of his achievement in 'Imaginary Elegies I–IV', he recognised that they were not what he was really aiming for, a serial poem, and while accepting that 'they're fine, they're very brilliant poems and technically they're lovely', he noted that 'they don't tell me very much more than what I knew when I was writing them, and that's the sign of, to me, a poem which is good but unsuccessful'.

Spicer's awareness that these 'Imaginary Elegies' were a start along that exploratory path which winds through the worlds of art and life is made succinctly clear in Section IV:

>   This much I've learned
> In these five years in what I spent and earned:
> Time does not finish a poem.
> The dummies in the empty funhouse watch
> The tides wash in and out. The thick old moon
> Shines through the rotten timbers every night.
> This much is clear, they think, the men who made
> Us twitch and creak and put the laughter in our throats
> Are just as cold as we. The lights are out.
>   The lights are out.

> You'll smell the oldest smells
> The smell of salt, of urine, and of sleep
> Before you wake. This much I've learned
> In these five years in what I've spent and earned:
> Time does not finish a poem.
> What have I gone to bed with all these years?
> What have I taken crying to my bed
> For love of me?
> Only the shadows of the sun and moon
> The dreaming groins, their creaking images.
> Only myself.

Andrew Crozier's interest in American poetry had of course been manifestly evident in his 1964 guest editorship of the American Supplement to *Granta*, and the absence of Spicer from that anthology was more to do with the editor's lack of knowledge of the latter's San Francisco address than with any lack of interest in his writing. This omission was put right soon after when Spicer's '15 False Propositions about God' appeared in the first issue of *The Wivenhoe Park Review*, Winter 1965. As for poems that 'echo and re-echo against each other', Crozier's interest in this idea was to form one of the central movements threading its way through both 'The Veil Poem' and the much later 'Free Running Bitch', which was first published in Iain Sinclair's 1996 anthology *Conductors of Chaos*.

Notes
1. *The Letters of John Keats*, ed. Hyder Edward Rollins (Cambridge University Press, 1958), p. 91.
2. Lewis Ellingham and Kevin Killian, *Poet Be Like God: Jack Spicer and the San Francisco Renaissance* (Wesleyan University Press, 1998), p. 96.
3. The quotations from Spicer's poems are taken from the admirable new edition of his work edited by Peter Gizzi and Kevin Killian and titled *my vocabulary did this to me: The Collected Poetry of Jack Spicer* (Wesleyan University Press, 2008).
4. Francis Ponge, *Oeuvres Complètes* (Gallimard, 1999), p. 29 (translation by Ian Brinton).
5. In *The House That Jack Built: The Collected Lectures of Jack Spicer*, ed. Peter Gizzi (Wesleyan University Press, 1998), p. 52.
6. *my vocabulary did this to me*, p. 133.

PETER BLAND

Wilderness Moments and Mr Maui

Wilderness Moments in Orange County

For Beryl

Between the taco stand and the used-car lot
on Santa Clara, there's that single patch
of date-palms where green parrots come
squawking to their nests high up
in those dried-out fronds. Such
wilderness moments, bordering the freeway,
relive themselves again and again
like the lone coyote
who kept strolling past Safeways
or that stranded whale among flustered sails
down at Marina-del-Rey. (Throw away
your *Moby-Dick*!) But it's mainly
the memory of those birds returning
with the sun going down like a nightly *Titanic*
and both of us clinging to that ache at dusk;
the first stars gathering much as those birds do
but silently… and further off.

Mr Maui's Monologues

Maui, the Maori trickster – half human, half god – was
crushed between the thighs of the Death Goddess while
entering her womb to create eternal life. Among his other
accomplishments he fished up the north island of New
Zealand, slowed down the sun, murdered his brother, and
decapitated several witches. Within the strict formalities of
Heaven and Earth he was generally regarded as something
of an outsider.

Mr Maui Looks Back

Increasingly I'm living in the past.
The local shaman puts it down to age,
a lost sense of belonging, the tribe
dispersed. We ate
pink mushrooms known as 'pearly gates'
and spoke to the spirit-world
about such things. But the dead
are less co-operative than they were
since we deserted tribal lands
and chose a more personal sense of quest.
Trapped on the borders between then and now
I've become a lengthening memory of myself.

Mr Maui Sees God in a Summer Garden

Summer: wombs are everywhere. They hang
as hives or quake underground.
God is a cannibal, but perfect… perfect…
spawning himself in jewelled shoals,
gorging among his seed-pods,
consuming himself in a variety of forms.

His sun-swarms gather… limbs, wings, and fins
ablaze in their elements. He's everywhere.
He eats his own sons. Crazed
with self-love he runs his disguises
down gyres and galaxies. He stamps and dances
through bee-filled branches
and the wormy corridors of fallen leaves.

Mr Maui Loses the Plot

I've forgotten the plot: birth, marriage, deaths,
a change of country, house, or sheets…
Surely that can't be all? The narrative
has quietly gone to pot
like me.
        Abandoned
I settle back to watch the tides
startle with their flash and suck.
Children cry… 'Surprise Surprise!'
and build a house out of light and mud.
I live like a hound growing fat on crumbs.
I hide under the table whenever the plot's discussed.

Mr Maui Among the Post-Modernists

Fuck it, don't turn away. *I AM*
as poor John Clare said,
hanging on by a hedgerow
when they put him
in his place. Even now
it's not a wilful subjectivity
but sheer survival… a clinging
to what's within reach.
        And so
go deconstruct yourselves, that's fine:
beautiful evasions, language games,
a sense of occasion, all pass the time
though lacking a certain urgency.
At least I'm in your face, an old
Aunt Sally or ventriloquist's doll
tied to a borrowed body, alive
to the voice that rattles in my head.

Mr Maui Turns Back to Vivaldi

On the box there's *another* serial killer.
Soon there'll be no-one left to kill.
How can evil be so numbingly boring?
I turn him off and go back
to Vivaldi…
            What a wanton thrill
to be out on the Tuscan hills again,
my feather cloak crackling in the autumn wind
and not a serial killer in sight
or none that I know save time itself.

Mr Maui at a Loss for Words

Nothing to say. That's why I'm saying it.
So where do we go from here?

Wet streets, bare beach, a winter pier.
Don't talk of belonging. This could be home.

Mr Maui Tries to Keep Fit

Twice round the park among the single mums,
stray dogs, and stroppy kids. Best done
at twilight or early dawn. Something
about the light, a crucial time, ends
and beginnings, what's come and gone
a hundred million trillion times
since one of us first stood up. Too late
to do more than gulp down air
after years of fear, blind
rage and lust. I've issued
a fatwah against those who've spilt
more blood than I ever could. Round
again, until the dark sees off
those dusky pinks that cling
to terraced streets. Now
the moon's out and I'm short of breath,
an overweight nomad, hands-on-hips,
travelling in circles round this small walled park
with all of time roaring inside my head.

Mr Maui Goes Global

God's dead. Old hat.
No joke. Take that.
Even Jacob's ladder
is going cheap. They sold
it at Sotheby's last week
for less than the cost
of a satellite dish. It's
good we're talking
to each other more
if only at a distance.
Borders were always
bad for business. They
kept us behind
closed doors. With
that in mind looking back
seems sad. So much
of it was unspeakably drab.
Only a rogue glance
when no one was looking
through office, classroom,
or factory window,
showed heaven was there
all the time. *Beautiful*
that's almost the only
word for it. Beam
me up Scotty, keep
the air-waves flowing.
I'm a New Age Gnostic
going global. Good
and evil have me
by the balls. When
they squeeze I repeat
– like Keats to his loved one –
beautiful, beautiful,
until it hurts.

Mr Maui at the Seaview Rest-Home

Just getting here has taken a lifetime.
Air's thinner, although scents linger.
There's the faintest whiff of childhood sands.
Steps limp down to the sea, but then
collapse in mid-air, going nowhere.

Choices here have been used up.

I must learn to keep my silences to myself
and only talk in whispers or small sobs,
being lost beyond words in some idiot joy
at the way these sunsets seem to last all day
and tides of light fill abandoned hulls.

MARK RYAN SMITH

Two Explorers: Charles Doughty and Hugh MacDiarmid

In Italy, towards the end of the 1940s, W.H. Auden met with his young typist James Schuyler. In his poem 'Wystan Auden', Schuyler describes what the older poet said to him:

> When he got off
> the liner at Naples, in black and
> a homburg, he said, 'I've just
> read *all* of Doughty's *The Dawn*
> *in Britain*.'

Further north and several decades earlier, two other poets were grappling with the same formidable work. Of an evening at Stone Cottage in Sussex, where Ezra Pound was working as secretary to W.B. Yeats, the American would read aloud to the Irishman, as recalled in Canto LXXXIII: 'did we ever get to the end of Doughty: / The Dawn in Britain? / perhaps not / Summons withdrawn, sir.)'. Auden's emphatic '*all*' wasn't possible for Pound and Yeats.

And, in 1933, in another cottage, this time in the tiny Shetland island of Whalsay, Hugh MacDiarmid wrote a little poem called 'To Charles Doughty', which includes this stanza:

> And slow as the movements
> O' continents in the sea
> Risin' and fallin' again
> Is your influence in me.

The journey from Naples to Stone Cottage to Whalsay is a journey which takes us from the cultural glut of a southern European city, into an austere and sometimes harsh northern landscape; from a place where many people have gone, to somewhere hardly anybody goes. And, just as Shetland is a place seldom ventured to, the formidable, eccentric, wholly individual, and ambitious work of Doughty is read by only a small number of hardy travellers.

Charles Montagu Doughty (1843–1926), despite the attention of MacDiarmid and others, is the great *terra incognita* of English literature. He is best remembered, if he is remembered at all, for his enormous prose work *Travels in Arabia Deserta* (1888), which recounts, in an elaborate and grand style, Doughty's years in the Arabian peninsula. Reading *Arabia Deserta* is a unique experience. As Doughty says in his preface, 'The book is not milk for babes: it might be likened to a mirror, wherein is set faithfully some parcel of the soil of Arabia smelling of sámn and camels'.

As well as writing one of the finest ever travel books, Doughty was also a poet. His poems, all of great length, were published between 1906 and 1923 and are all, to use Pound's phrase, resolutely 'out of key with their times'. In *The Dawn in Britain*, a six-volume epic dealing with the early history of the British isles, we find lines like these:

> Now, after sundered from the Continent;
> This Isle lay empty, a land of cloud and frost,
> And forest of wild beasts; till creeping time
> Brought man's kin forth. Then Fathers of the World,
> Begate the nations. Last few fisher folk,
> Passed, driven by tempest, from the Mainland's coast.
> They feeble of stature, clad in fells of beasts;
> (Whose weapons, in their hands, were sharp flint stones,)
> The river strands possessed, and wild salt shores.
> To them were holes, delved underground, for bowers:
> Trees were and streams and hills and stars, their gods.

This was first published in 1906. Doughty was an Old Testament prophet in the age of the wireless, a Spenserian epic poet in the era of the moving picture. He is an anachronistic figure in a rapidly changing literary world but, as we have seen, he was also a presence for some of the major poets of the modern era.

Doughty's influence on MacDiarmid began risin' and fallin' at around the same time the poet moved to Shetland. As is well known, he arrived in the isles, in 1932, at a time of great personal turmoil and, if the life of Chris Grieve was a difficult one in the 1930s (he suffered a nervous breakdown in 1935), much of the writing he did in Shetland has proved difficult for readers to love. His early Scots lyrics, his extraordinary clamjamfry *A Drunk Man Looks at a Thistle*, and his masterpiece 'On a Raised Beach' (which does belong to the Shetland period) all occupy high places in the MacDiarmid canon. But his poetry from the mid-30s onwards – 'the problem of the immense, Siberian tundra of the later works', as Michael Schmidt puts it – is seen rather less affectionately. MacDiarmid's work in this later period, much of which was written as part of a gigantic, never-realised, epic work titled *Mature Art*, is, it must be said, often difficult, sometimes tedious, arcane, and overly verbose. But is also a poetry with the most serious aims and aspirations. When it clicks into gear, as it does more often than its detractors might allow, the verse can emerge from a series of multiple esoteric digressions into something exhilarating and full of a compelling life-force, as we see here in *In Memoriam James Joyce*:

> Ah, Joyce, this is our task
> Making what a moving, thrilling, mystical, tropical,
> Maniacal, magical creation of all these oppositions,
> Of good to evil, greed to self-sacrifice,
> Selfishness to selflessness, of this all-pervading
>   atmosphere,
> Of the seen merging with the unseen,
> Of the beautiful sacrificed to the ugly,
> Of the ugly transformed to the beautiful,
> Of this intricate yet always lucid and clear-sighted
> Agglomeration of passions, manias, occult influences,

Historical and classical references
– Sombre, insane, brilliant and sane...

But, despite the thrill of such passages, the later poetry remains problematic. Readers haven't quite got to grips with what MacDiarmid was doing in these works, preferring the mysteriousness and brilliance of 'The Watergaw' or 'The Eemis Stane' to the slowly moving agglomerations of *In Memoriam James Joyce* or *The Kind of Poetry I Want*.

In a letter to Edith Trelease Aney in 1952 MacDiarmid wrote:

> Finally you ask what poet has influenced me most. That is a difficult question to answer. I am not easily influenced. I have read enormously and known many great poets of many lands, but I think I have not been influenced directly very much, though of course I have learned technical devices and found myself impelled towards certain types of subject matter and forms of treatment by many very diverse poets, e.g. Yeats, Pound, Hopkins, Rilke, Rimbaud, Mayakovsky. Probably the best answer to your question is Doughty.

In a poet, and a man, so independently minded as MacDiarmid, the question of influence is not an easy one, but by drawing parallels between him and Doughty we can perhaps move towards a greater appreciation of what MacDiarmid was trying to do in his later work.

In the first few years of his Shetland sojourn, MacDiarmid produced one of his key volumes, *Stony Limits and Other Poems* (1934), which contains 'On a Raised Beach'. In the book, that great poem follows a sequence of three elegies: to Scottish nationalist Liam Mac'Ille Iosa, to Rainer Maria Rilke, and finally to Doughty. The Doughty poem, which MacDiarmid considered one of his best, contains these lines:

> I know how on turning to noble hills
> And stark deserts happily still preserved
> For men whom no gregariousness fills
> With the loneliness for which they are nerved
> – The lonely at-one-ment with all worth while –
> I can feel as if the landscape and I
> Became each other and see my smile
> In the corners of the vastest contours lie
> And share the gladness and peace you knew,
> – The supreme human serenity that was you!

In the first line of his elegy to Rilke – 'Halophilous living by these far northern seas' – MacDiarmid arrives on the Shetland coast, and these lines in the Doughty poem see him pushing further into the stony, austere landscape which surrounded him in the islands. The poem ends with a startling image of MacDiarmid sitting next to Doughty's skull, 'whose emptiness is worth / The sum of almost all the full heads now on Earth'. Passing from this image of the skull to the famous opening lines of 'On a Raised Beach' completes the poet's journey into the Shetland landscape, penetrating deep into the geological layers that have formed over many centuries. By passing through the symbolically important figure of Doughty, MacDiarmid can find his way into the stones on that beach on the little island of Linga. By taking up a vantage point from next to Doughty's empty skull, MacDiarmid could write that he was 'enamoured of the desert at last'.

A year before he died, MacDiarmid was interviewed for BBC Radio Scotland by George Bruce. When asked about 'On a Raised Beach' he said:

> I was trying to define my own position generally in terms of my environment at that time which was the Shetland Islands where, of course, geology is the prominent feature. You've got none of the resources for illustrative material you'd have on the mainland of Scotland. There are no trees, no running water. You're thrown back on the bare rock all the time. So I was trying to re-shape my ideas of poetry, identifying myself in terms of the Shetland landscape. That's what I was doing. I think it's one of my very best poems, either in Scots or English.

Doughty studied geology at Cambridge, going on to do fieldwork on a glacier in Norway (did he, perhaps, pass through Shetland on his way there?), and in *Arabia Deserta* this interest is apparent on almost every page. He goes amongst nomadic tribes, often risking his life, but he also pushes deep into the barren landscape surrounding him:

> We look out from every height, upon the Harra, over an iron desolation; what uncouth blackness and lifeless cumber of vulcanic matter! – a hard-set face of nature without a smile for ever, a wilderness of burning and rusty horror of unformed matter. What lonely life would not feel constraint of heart to trespass here! the barren heaven, the nightmare soil! where should he look for comfort?

MacDiarmid's raised beach is more hopeful than Doughty's iron desolation, but there are parallels to be drawn here. Doughty's position as an outsider in Arabia – as a Christian, as a lettered man among illiterate people – must have struck a chord with MacDiarmid in Whalsay. But, more importantly, the two writers both push themselves into the harsh rock and spartan landscapes of Shetland and Arabia to produce works of very considerable stature.

If the poetry produced in MacDiarmid's first few years in Shetland represents, in part, a symbolic journey into the landscape, the poems from the *Mature Art* period move in a rather different direction. The triumph of 'On a Raised Beach' is that, as well as being a very locatable poem, it is a poem which ranges spiritually and philosophically far. It is both very local and very expansive. The later poems cannot be located in the same way, either in terms of the landscape or in terms of the poetic persona we find in them.

In Memoriam James Joyce, published as a single work in 1955, can be taken as paradigmatic of MacDiarmid's later epic poetry. In it we encounter a bewildering range of references – from Indian literature to Shetland's ancient Norn language, with innumerable stops in between. This is big poetry. It is a poetry which moves very far from the small island MacDiarmid was living in when he wrote it; a place, we should remember, with no libraries or centres of learning anywhere near. This writing isn't to everybody's taste, but the simple fact that it was written, in the place it was written, is an achievement in itself.

On the surface, there seem few points of correspondence between the epic verse of MacDiarmid and that of Doughty: Doughty is archaic, MacDiarmid incorporates modern scientific terminology; Doughty's poems are narrative, MacDiarmid's are not. But, in what their poetry seeks to accomplish, we can perhaps see what MacDiarmid drew from his predecessor. What both men were tilting at was nothing less than both the reinvention of the English language, *and* a wholesale reassessment of what the poet's position in the world should be. Neither Doughty nor MacDiarmid ever set his sights low.

In different ways, both poets are reacting against the same thing: what they perceived as the degeneracy of the English language of their day. In the 'Post Illa' to *The Dawn in Britain*, Doughty sets out what he saw as the poet's responsibility to the language:

> it is the prerogative of every lover of his Country, to use the instrument of his thought, which is the Mother-tongue, with propriety and distinction; to keep that reverently clean and bright, which lies at the root of his mental life, and so, by extension, of the life of the Community: putting away all impotent and disloyal vility of speech, which is no uncertain token of a people's decadence.

Doughty saw the English of his day as being an atrophied shadow of a language which had reached an early high point in Chaucer (in Arabia, to save luggage space, Doughty buried a number of books but retained his volume of Chaucer), and had found its most brilliant form of expression with Spenser. By harking back to these poets, Doughty thought, his poems could rediscover the grandeur the language had once displayed.

MacDiarmid's tangle with the English language is also a reaction against what he saw as a degeneracy. In his 1931 essay 'English Ascendancy in British Literature', MacDiarmid argues powerfully for a poetry which includes all kinds of non-standard languages and suggests that, because of the oppressive imperial position of England within the British Isles, these minority tongues cannot be heard. But MacDiarmid had already done his great work in Scots and, in his later epic poetry, instead of developing a 'minority' voice further, he writes in English. The crucial thing is, however, that his English is a thoroughly *deterritorialised* English. It is not the narrow standardised English of the imperial ascendancy, but a language which seeks to range through the world and through the languages of the world. Again, from the interview with Bruce, when asked why he started to write in English, MacDiarmid said:

> I was becoming increasingly preoccupied with political and scientific matters, and there was no vocabulary for them in Scots. There's no vocabulary in English either; you had to use the international scientific jargon, you see, which I did use.

Just as he had done in his Scots poetry, MacDiarmid refuses to limit his language to place. An imperially imposed language, a language of one place forced on another, is a provincial language (in the sense that it refuses to accept the 'minority' tongue as valid) and, in his attempt to create an English language fit for a poetry which encompasses the whole world, MacDiarmid was reacting against that provincialism. Doughty looked back, MacDiarmid looked forward, but they both aimed at nothing less than creating anew the English language they found themselves facing in the first few decades of the century.

The two poets also converge in terms of what they saw as the place of the poet in society. If they are both reacting against the state of the language, they are also both reacting against a poetry which proceeds from the self. Both Doughty and the later MacDiarmid move far from the Romantic notion that poetry is about individual self-expression or the overflow of personal emotion or feeling. In *The Dawn in Britain* especially, Doughty seeks to provide a unifying series of national myths. But, according to another of Doughty's modern advocates, he goes even further than this. Laura Riding, in her introduction to a never-published Carcanet volume of Doughty's work, writes:

> Doughty tried to bring poetry within the frame of cosmic actuality as the setting of human actuality. Poetry, for Doughty, made possible the use of language for the spiritual deciphering of human existence – *and* of the essential phenomena of being, as viewed with poetic vision.

Doughty is concerned not with his own being in the world and what that might mean, but with the world, with human existence and with being itself. He is not interested in a poetry which emerges from the subjective consciousness of the poet, but is attempting to write a large-scale, unifying poetry which strives to unravel the big and difficult questions humanity has faced for centuries.

MacDiarmid's epic poetry, like Doughty's, does not flow from a subjective Romantic sensibility, but takes for its subject, very simply, everything. It is a poetry which seeks to unify the diversity of existence within its enormous frame. *In Memoriam James Joyce* invokes Doughty early on:

> Doughty, by far the greatest of them all,
> Infinite in his awareness and charity,
> Harbinger of the epical age of Communism

As MacDiarmid argues in his 1936 pamphlet *Charles Doughty and the Need for Heroic Poetry*, it is epic (as opposed to subjective, bourgeois lyric) which is best suited to Communist society. Communism, for MacDiarmid, was a utopian, unifying system, and the kind of epic poetry he wrote from the mid-30s onwards seeks to create an inclusive, synthesising, utopian space in which the entire world can be incorporated. It is a poetry which is infinitely varied but a poetry which also aims for the impossible, unattainable, omnific One. The poet's responsibility is not to express himself, but to grapple with the world in all its wonderful enormous babbling clamour. In a multifarious world, MacDiarmid saw poetry as the most powerful force for unity. Again, from the interview with Bruce, when MacDiarmid was asked what mattered to him, he replied:

> Poetry matters. I regard poetry as one of the things that matters most in the world. The organic apprehension that can only be achieved through poetry seems to me sadly lacking. There has been a playing down of the increasing complexity and pace of modern life and so on, playing down the role of the imagination. The seer, the fore-knower, has been displaced in a hierarchy of human beings. It requires to be replaced there.

Both MacDiarmid and Doughty considered the task of the poet as being one of unification. The poet could unite a nation, could bring together the world, and, for both men, poetry was the central force in society. For Doughty and MacDiarmid, explorers both, poetry, more than anything else, was able to attempt a 'spiritual deciphering of human existence', not from the starting point of a single subjective consciousness, but by crossing boundaries, by ranging out and moving through time, by venturing far and deep into the universe and all it contains.

Mark Ryan Smith: Two Explorers: Charles Doughty and Hugh MacDiarmid

MAKING NEW THE WORD-HOARD

The Word Exchange: Anglo-Saxon Poems in Translation, edited by Greg Delanty and Michael Matto (Norton) £25

This book is one of those projects that work so well you wonder why it has not been done before. The editors have selected a large body of the shorter poems in Old English and printed their texts faced by new translations by what Michael Matto calls 'a panoply of voices', drawing on a considerable number of the leading current poets in English from both sides of the Atlantic. That is an achievement in itself: it is unusual to have transatlantic poets appearing in the same context at all; indeed they often hardly know of each other's existence. But the primary achievement of this superb book is to provide an anthology of these great poems together, alongside distinguished modern versions in verse. Every poetry enthusiast is aware of notable translations of the Anglo-Saxon poems – by Longfellow, Pound, Auden, Heaney, Edwin Morgan; but there has never been a major attempt to represent something approaching the whole corpus in verse translations. From the 30,000-odd surviving lines of Anglo-Saxon verse, space is made for the range of *The Word Exchange* by leaving out *Beowulf* (Heaney's will do, under separate cover). The major Biblical poems of the Junius manuscript are largely absent, as are some heroic poems, such as the two 'Guthlac's'. But what survives gives a remarkably good sense of the tone and concerns of this major poetic corpus.

After an elegant brief 'Foreword' by Seamus Heaney, celebrating 'the ongoing vitality of Anglo-Saxon poetry a millennium after its demise might have been expected' (and nearly a century, one is tempted to add, after its demise began to be wished for in some quarters), Greg Delanty's 'Preface' explains the conception of the book, and Michael Matto's 'Introduction' proper introduces the corpus, drawing on some of the book's translators. At the end, a few of the translators explain what drew them to choose the poems they translate here. In between, the main body of the book is divided into fourteen sections: nearly all the *Exeter Book Riddles* are here, elegantly arranged as seven 'Riddle-Hoards', alternating with seven other categories: 'Poems of Exile and Longing' – the six great 'elegies'; 'Poems about Historical Battles, People, and Places'; 'Poems about Living'; 'Poems about Dying'; 'Biblical Stories and Lives of Saints'; 'Prayers, Admonitions and Allegories'; and 'Remedies and Charms'.

A great virtue of the diversity here is that the translating poets can play to their own strengths. A poem like 'The Wanderer' (translated with an earnest focus here by Delanty himself) has a richness of thought that admits of several kinds of poem in its translation. The same is true of a poem like 'Wulf and Eadwacer' (if there is any other poem like it), perhaps the most commonly translated Anglo-Saxon poem in recent years. Here its wily crypticism is translated by Paul Muldoon: the perfect poet for such an elusive piece, you would have thought. In fact Muldoon uses a kind of graceful, flat, Irish plainstyle for it:

How very differently it goes for us...
It was after my far-flung Wulf I was sighing
as the rain came down and my tears flowed
when a hard man took me under his wing...

Also in the first section – 'Exile and Longing' – Heaney translates 'Deor' in a version that makes a fine appendix to his *Beowulf*:

Her love was her bane,   it banished sleep.
   That passed over,   this can too.

Derek Mahon's two translations – 'Durham' and 'The Kentish Hymn' – both display his trademark classical grace. Another of the best things in the opening section is Michael Schmidt's version of 'The Husband's Message', a poem which traditionally has been found difficult to place generically between elegy, riddle, prayer or inscription. Schmidt repairs the lacunas in the opening lines with total conviction:

I remain true   to the tree I was hacked from
Wood I am, bearing   the marks of a man
Letters and runes   the words of his heart

This illustrates one of the many crucial formal decisions the modern translators have to make. Are they to keep the gaps in the original, or to propose a repair? The editors sometimes help by sternly printing manuscript emendations in bold in the original. Mary Jo Salter, in her beautifully spare version of 'The Seafarer', does the same as Schmidt, so that the wrinkles around lines 112–13 are unnoticeable. David Constantine in Riddle 84 honours the lacunas completely. Matthew Hollis omits the caesuras but keeps the breaks in his admirable 'Waldere A and B' in a way that maintains the poem's total coherence:

   ...no better blade,
save one, in my own keeping,
sleeping in its sheath.

The modern reader might not expect to find imagistic brilliance amongst the moralising wisdom poems such as 'The Maxims'. But listen to Brigit Pegeen Kelly's beginning to her translation of 'Maxims 1 – B':

Frost must freeze, fire melt wood,
   earth bear fruit, ice build bridges,
and, most wonderful, water put on a glass helmet
   to protect the earth's sprouts.

On the basis of these last two examples, it is tempting to generalise and say that the removal of the caesura is a good tactic: but generalisations are dangerous in this formally diverse field.

Kelly's third line recalls one of the most wonderful of the riddles, number 69 (unimprovably translated by Kevin Crossley-Holland in his Penguin edition: 'On the way a miracle: water become bone'). Here Jennifer Grotz links it to number 68 (as many do). The treatment of the riddles in *The Word Exchange* is inexhaustibly interesting, particularly in the treatment of meaning – an even more crucial decision of course for the translator: how faithful to be to the meaning of the original (always assuming we can be sure what exactly that is). The question is whether the translator is producing a new poem. This is wonderfully done in some surprising places: in 'Bede's Death Song' by Anthony Cronin for example: 'For when that hour arrives / It will be too late / To add or subtract, / Regret or amend.' But the question of fidelity arises most crucially in the riddles. There are two obvious ways to treat them. One is to deduce what the answer to the riddle is and then make a translation on that subject. That has been the normal practice and it often works well. But often the proposed answer has been too general – the several 'Creation' poems for example (and for what it is worth, I think that answer is wrong in all cases; something like 'Nature' seems better). The second way is for the modern poet to respond to the words of the original without being restricted to the theme of the 'answer'. This seems better to me; for exemplary instances, look at David Constantine's versions of riddles 30 and 41, and Gary Soto's translation of 'The Rake' riddle (number 34). Constantine's beautiful rendition of number 41 (usually rather feebly glossed as 'Water') lets the poem do the work of suggestion, maintaining the opening lacuna:

> ...but when
> Renewal comes she visits us here
> In many appearances, bright dark,

before concluding menacingly 'Understand this / Or die'.

Finally, it is only fair to note that many of the longer translations are also very good – Maurice Riordan's extract from 'Soul and Body I' for example. I want to finish with what I think is the finest thing in the book – something which is a new masterpiece, again found in an unobvious place: David Ferry's 'Offering of Isaac' from *Genesis A*. Translating the Old English alliterative lines into a series of graceful couplets, Ferry captures this terrible episode with haunting force:

> "Abraham, Abraham, you
> Must take your beloved child,
> Your own, your only son...
> And kill him with its edge,
> And burn his dear body black."

Not surprisingly, Ferry's note on his choice of this text is the most impressive of the translators' notes at the end. But it is only one of the compelling virtues of this truly wonderful book.

BERNARD O'DONOGHUE

POETRY SEARCHES FOR RADIANCE

ADAM ZAGAJEWSKI, *Selected Poems*, translated by Clare Cavanagh, Renata Gorczynski, Benjamin Ivry and C.K. Williams (Faber) £12.99
ADAM ZAGAJEWSKI, *Eternal Enemies*, translated by Clare Cavanagh (Farrar, Straus and Giroux) $14.00
ADAM ZAGAJEWSKI, *Unseen Hand*, translated by Clare Cavanagh (Farrar, Straus and Giroux) $23.00

Titles have a poetry of their own. *Eternal Enemies* refers to Zagajewski's 'Epithalamium' (for Isca and Sebastian): 'Only in marriage do love and time, / eternal enemies, join forces'. Time, with its companions loss and death, plays a central role in Zagajewski's poems. The changing seasons, dawn and dusk, past history, the decline of cities, all furnish the imagery that fuels the pervasive melancholy of his beautifully observed tributes to persons and places. As for love – it is the great reconciler, the motive force of hope, life itself.

Eternal Enemies is dedicated 'To Maya, *toujours*', and her presence is felt throughout, in 'Music Heard' and 'Music Heard with You', in remembered quarrels, estrangement, moments of joy. Most of the poems are autobiographical, a poet's life distilled to a fleeting moment, an emotion shadowed by its opposite. An early 'Self-Portrait' is qualified ironically by a second, 'Self-Portrait: Not Without Doubts': 'Enthusiasm moves you in the morning, / by evening you lack the nerve / even to glance at the blackened page'.

I met Zagajewski in his beloved Krakow, the 'gray and lovely city' to which he has returned after years of self-imposed exile in Paris. We had lunch in an ancient restaurant, looking out through a driving rain on the medieval Market Square – Adam, his wife Maya, and I. I felt as if I already knew Adam through his poems, in which he appears as a solitary wanderer, a traveller to far-flung places, a detached observer of ordinary life, anchored in history; a seeker after truth, happiness, 'radiance'.

But it was a different Adam who made the stronger impression on me: Adam watching Maya with love, as she talked to me about her longing to return to Paris and the impossibility of doing so. I suddenly understood her presence in the poems. 'Carrots, onions, celery, prunes, almonds, powdered sugar, four large apples, green are best (your love letter)' ('Antennas in the Rain'); 'We quarreled here once, do you remember...' ('Morning'); 'We met for the first time that year' ('1969'); 'I love gazing at my wife's face' ('Self-Portrait'); 'I thought about you, about us, / about sharp and shining moments / plucked from my imagination like a thorn / drawn from an athlete's narrow foot' ('For M.').

Maya is the anchor for the poet's restless wanderings, his sense of emptiness, nothingness, the despair inseparable from the history that is never very far away in these poems, the fate of the Jews, dictators and generals, their hapless victims. The few explicitly political poems are as powerful for our troubled age as Auden is for his: 'Bent under burdens which sometimes / can be seen and sometimes can't, / they trudge through mud or desert sands, / hunched, hungry... It could be Bosnia today, / Poland in September '39, France / eight months later, Germany in '45, / Somalia, Afghanistan, Egypt' ('Refugees'). Indeed, Zagajewski is best-known for the poem which *The New Yorker* put on its back cover after 9/11, 'Try to Praise the Mutilated World': 'You must praise the mutilated world... You should praise the mutilated world... Praise the mutilated world / and the gray feather a thrush lost, / and the gentle light that strays and vanishes / and returns'.

Czesław Miłosz introduced Zagajewski to an English-speaking readership with words of high praise: 'What a joy to see a major poet emerging from a mass of contemporaries and taking the lead in the poetry of my language...' Like Miłosz, Zagajewski opposes the savage events of recent history with the effort to hold onto ordinary life, and the fragile evidence of man's capacity to create beauty, in music, painting, the difficult art of poetry. His poems can be read as word-paintings: scenes and images arranged with apparent artlessness, inviting the reader to share the writer's elegiac vision and his persistent questioning of meaning, design, the 'unseen hand' of his most recent collection.

Zagajewski was born in 1945, and for him, as for Miłosz, the horrors of the war are ever-present. After the war his family was moved from Lvov, ceded to the Soviet Union, to the industrial city of Gliwice, in Silesia. He grew up with an abiding hatred of its ugliness, and escaped at eighteen to study in Krakow. The medieval city had been almost untouched by war, except for the

Jewish quarter of Kazimierz, from which thousands of Jews were deported to Auschwitz. Now a tourist destination, Auschwitz is a recurrent 'absent presence' in the poems: 'The Swallows of Auschwitz'; 'Unwritten Elegy for Krakow's Jews' ('in the evening shadows gather here from every neighbourhood, / and even some brought by trains from nearby towns').

In the 1970s, Zagajewski became part of the opposition, wrote leaflets, signed manifestos, until he was drawn first to West Berlin, then to Paris and Maya – not a political but an 'erotic' exile, as he told an interviewer. In Paris he found his true voice as a poet, and also as a persona or speaker, the solitary walker in the city, the 'I' who observes, experiences, 'listens to music a little, reads a little', always a sceptical outsider, seeking a truth which forever escapes him.

Unseen Hand, like *Eternal Enemies*, offers elegiac descriptions of incidents, places, times and persons observed, remembered, or almost wholly imagined, as in an earlier poem, 'To Go to Lvov' (his lost birthplace). Organised like a sonata in three sections with overlapping themes, there are memories of the poet's childhood in Gliwice, more ironic 'Self-Portraits', moving poems about his father, suffering irreversible loss of memory (in an earlier poem: 'I ask my father: "What do you do all day?" "I remember"'). There are sequences of word-paintings (reminiscent of still lifes, or Monet's series of poplars, haystacks, Rouen Cathedral): modernity ('Self-Portrait in an Airplane, in economy class'), inevitable decline (Joseph Street, in the Kazimierz, populated only by the dead), counterpointed with 'The lovely Garonne, which passes through drowsy villages each night / like a priest with the last sacrament…'

Zagajewski has written autobiographical essays which fill out his intellectual and political history, explaining his beliefs or the impossibility of belief; and he has another life, teaching as a member of the Committee on Social Thought at the University of Chicago. But the poems stand on their own, elusive and oblique, sometimes no more than jottings in a notebook, single germs of poems, developed with an artist's hand into a wonderful variety of formal portraits, self-portraits, elegies and meditations.

Although Faber published *Selected Poems* a few years ago, the most recent collections are available only in the United States. They should most certainly be made available here. I felt when I first read them the excitement of discovering a voice that spoke of one's own most pressing concerns – how to live, how to make sense of history, of loss, of love.

JUDITH CHERNAIK

FACTS AND TRUTH

DAN BURT, *Certain Windows* (Lintott Press) £9.95

The centrepiece of Dan Burt's second Lintott chapbook collection is a tense, often brilliant prose-memoir of his formative years in the post-war, working-class, Jewish district of South Philadelphia. In particular, it is a portrait of his parents, Joe Burt, the youngest son of a carpenter from the Pale, and Louise Kevitch, the daughter of 'tough Jews' who ran the Tenderloin's numbers racket and its associated prostitution, gambling and protection operations for half a century until the action moved to Atlantic City.

Our sympathies are subtly but firmly directed towards Joe, a brawler and semi-pro boxer whose fights seem emblematic of a wider social and ethnic struggle for survival. 'Lust and rage beset his every age', the author writes, with a feeling mixture of revulsion and pride, before reassuring us that 'bullies and every form of authority were [his father's] targets'. At the age of ten, he fells a lout with a lead pipe. Scarred by the Depression, Joe drops out of school (his brother stays on), becomes a butcher, struggles to keep the family business afloat, but is saved by war-time trade and the deals he cuts with black-market slaughterhouses. Justice is rough. When an anti-profiteering inspector asks to see the coupons for the meat being sold, Joe pitches him through a plate-glass window. When Louise stalls the car in front of a tram and the tram driver insults her 'sex, intelligence and parents', Joe runs to the tram, hauls out the driver and beats him unconscious. A lot of this instinctive, retributive violence is complicated, and in part explained, by its proximity to the Kevitches, a clan of Jacobean monstrosities – and murderers – from whom Joe does his best to shield Dan, but on whom, of course, the family also relies to get Joe off the hook after the defenestration; to pay off the IRS, to 'protect' its own faltering respectability. They are a frankly terrifying crowd, shooting state legislators, gunning down delinquents, denying everything, and their mad annexation of mob loyalty to aspirationalism is contagious, so that when Joe finally wins $250 in a crap game and blows it all on a model train set for his two boys, Dan and Rick, we sense the gesture's doubleness, the guilt behind the sudden, jarring generosity.

Some of that doubleness also blurs the otherwise transparent style of *Certain Windows*. It is a striking account of intimidation and struggle, for the most part simply told, which would come over as plainly true were it not for Burt's odd, pre-emptive strike against doubters at the outset: the 'dishonesty and danger of romantic reconstruction', he says, 'is reason enough to try and record as accurately as possible what we saw, if we record at all'. It is as if he does not quite believe it all himself, and gives his tale a hint of those *voyages extraordinaires* whose narrating witnesses, like Watson in the Holmes stories, are always astonished into reporting the wild facts. At the end, too, after a thrilling and moving last chapter devoted to Joe's second career as a Jersey coast charter captain, the author tells us that his purpose has been to find out 'how vision forms, how I come to understand what I do of the world and whether that understanding is sound'. But it isn't certain that this is what he has done, and there is some collapsing of categories here. The birth of the adult artist is missing from these pages. Why did the scion of mobsters and a poor meat-trader become a poet? Impossible to tell. Why did he also become a very successful lawyer and high-finance businessman?

That much we may deduce.

For the facts, we have a prose recollection; for the truth, or for invention that is true, we turn to the poems that bookend the pamphlet, and which variously foreshadow and echo its themes of brutality and loss. Burt is a painstaking and able poet; all of the verse in *Certain Windows* is enjoyable, and some of it exceptional. The commemorations of Louise ('Death Mask') and Joe ('Ishmael', 'Who He Was', 'Trade'), as of the wider American-Jewish experience of self-definition ('John Winthrop's Ghost'), are formal and learned – but their wealth of allusion, to the myth of Tereus and Procne, to Spartan mothers, to the Old Testament and the authoritarian early history of Massachusetts, never seems forced. They are a part of the 'vision' and a proof of Empson's chatty but shrewd theory that 'the reason for writing verse is to clear your own mind and fix your feelings'.

The best poem is called 'Rosebud', after the totemic sled, and uses Burt's favourite, Tennysonian tetrameter – a tricky rhythm, because it only *seems* innocent and therefore inclines either to false naivety or irony – to revisit his father's tenderness. It is a fine narrative elegy, an act of filial invocation couched inside the story of how young Dan coveted and was given a Raleigh bike for his birthday, only to lose it at once:

> So long a dream it slipped my mind
> Till I walked back to school at nine
> And saw it hanging, bent, flensed,
> A skeleton on the school fence

Into those simple stresses the verse packs a world of wartime horror, already past but not yet conceivable from the child's point of view. It's delicately done. The boy goes home, bikeless, fears punishment and lies awake all night. In the morning, Joe 'shook me, eyes red / Free from my twisted covers / To find a second virgin racer'. At this point, Burt relaxes his grip on the meter, its stresses bounced farther apart in longer lines, and with that relaxation comes the right kind of doubleness, for which one feels the poet has long been reaching and searching, and by which he is rewarded – a lovely accuracy of emotional statement that comprehends mystery without trying to understand it:

> We never spoke about those Raleighs.
> Perhaps my desolation recalled the
> Depression corner where he hawked apples
> with his father, memory of an older brother
> pedalling past to high school while he walked
> to work, or something from his favourite film,
> *Citizen Kane*. Now I cannot know. Old myself,
> when I survey the wreck we make of life
> he comes to mind and the vessel rights:
> in balance with what's worst, two bikes.

WILL EAVES

FROM TABBINISI

ED REISS, *Your Sort* (Smith/Doorstop Books) £9.95

Hakagawa, Eliot's character who was 'bowing among the Titians', seems at home in drawing-rooms, but Ed Reiss looks for a wife for him from the trawler fishing industry.

> I'm looking for a mate for Hakagawa.
> She'd better have a quirky sense of humour:
> some go-getter from the frontier:
>
> Kirsty McDougall, radio-operator
> Kariann Kiehl, gillnetter-skipper
> Ardel Krogh, patrolling the marina
>
> Sockeye Sue Hahn, Enforcement Officer
> who leaps aboard a suspect trawler
> skidding down the deck on fish-slime.
> …
>
> or Joan Skogan
> who monitors by-catch, offal, quotas
> close to screaming high-speed filleting machines
>
> in the guts of the factory-ship
> where people are good and kind to one another.
> She might be a mate for Hakagawa.

Reiss is at his best in this poem from his first full collection: wit and whimsicality are joined with fellow-feeling and a fathom-deep interest in others. Two-thirds of the poems are about other people (a relief when so many poets are unsparingly interested in themselves). Among the characters are a celebrity Zeus who's working on his issues, a tour guide to Roman mosaics (with comic English), Harold Godwinson as a schoolboy, Aunt May who had tinkers in for tea, and a woman obsessed with Norman Tebbit's fingers. Reiss has particular sympathy for disturbed outsiders; the speaker in 'Suspended' is ejected from an art gallery for kneeling down, and ends up in Tesco's (with its background music):

> Billy Joel. Olive oil.
> All shall be fulfilled.
> Standing in the poultry aisle
> I heard my name proclaim'd.

I'm less convinced, however, by some archetypal, eccentric Yorkshire 'characters' whom Reiss creates and inhabits, such as 'Appy Arry' and 'Badger Bill'; their folksiness is offered as an end in itself, without wider significance.

The variety of Reiss's subjects extends to bumblebees, broken umbrellas, Englishness, and evolution. His interest in religion encompasses controversies in Judaism and a miracle in Islam. Personal poems are relatively few, but I am moved by a father-son conversation in 'Odd' and by the love affair in 'Homage to Hieronymus Bosch'. This poet is widely informed: there are literary allusions ranging from Shakespeare and Milton to Hughes and Heaney, and cultural references to the Bible, the mythical Buddhist kingdom of Shambhala, ankle-tagging, and credit derivatives. Reiss has considerable tonal variety; there are humour, irony, satire and self-deprecation alongside the different voices and idiolects. The diversity of this collection makes the whole greater than the sum of its parts; it has many dimensions in a little space.

Reiss is also versatile with forms and stanzas: there are sonnets in many shapes, two sestinas, an excellent pantoum. The imperfect rhyme used in some poems is unobtrusive and satisfying. I'm much taken by the extended conceits: a school of social sciences is like a Gnostic community at Tabbinisi in Roman Egypt; a lover has built up his beloved's name into an abbey in a park, which falls into ruin. I like the occasional puns and linguistic games: 'no hand has seen, no eye has heard'.

The author's reticence extends to the back cover, where his biography is five words long. As for the author's 'photograph' – look at the beautiful front cover, which is a detail from a painting by Bosch, and find in the bottom right-hand corner an anxious lover looking over his shoulder at you.

The collection is framed by poems about a tadpole. In the very first poem, 'Upstart', a tadpole tries to climb Mount Everest. In the middle of the book the tadpole realises he's on the wrong mountain; he should be climbing Parnassus. The last poem, 'Vanity of Vanities', is just three lines:

> Super-tadpole drops
> petal from Parnassus. Waits
> to hear an echo.

The tadpole is altogether too modest. Ed Reiss has produced a collection of compassionate, funny, wry, thoughtful, economic, lovingly made poems.

CHRIS PREDDLE

AN ORIGINAL UNDER THE LID

IAN POPLE, *Saving Spaces* (Arc Publications) £7.99

Although the title of Ian Pople's third book may not be a promising introduction – hovering as it does between semi-religious banality and daytime television-programme title – it does pose a question which refracts interestingly over Pople's poetry. 'Saving Spaces', as a phrase, is intriguingly ambiguous between describing the act of a person in preserving a place, and, alternatively, describing the offering, by a place, of some protective consolation. Given that Carol Rumens has noted how Pople's writing tends to come with a 'theological framework' which is 'extra-poetic' (here with a raft of biblical epigraphs and titular reference), there must be a reserve, then, about how much work the poems expect to pass off onto their surroundings. Might they seem dependent on the shelter of faith as a kind of well of ready-made profundity, or is the poetry – as in the former interpretation of the book's title – capable of nourishing its own wellsprings of meaning?

At their best, Pople's words can conjure acutely vivid spaces:

> You were running over snow,
> snow over the playing field.
> Your feet were kicking up
>
> snow in arcs from your heels.

(from 'The Bleachers')

The repetition and geometric imagery creates an enclosed dramatic arena from which Pople can suddenly move outward:

> ... grey skies
> over bleachers, those skies
> over concert halls, listening
>
> to the end of the cadenza,
> to the gathering applause,
> the applause ending.

This assertion of the relation between things – between scales of time and space, between sensory modalities, between atmospheres – is something Pople does extraordinarily well. The short opening poems of the book tend to feature almost pastorally gentle English countrysides, suddenly interrupted by the bustlings and absurdities of humanity – the relief of finished business, the inexplicable and fleeting thought – which somehow works to affirm how *amongst* it all we are. Jen Hadfield's T.S. Eliot Prize-winning *Nigh-No-Place* repeatedly utilises a similar effect.

The longer, sequential poems later in the book, though, seem to take for granted a kind of protective buffer of poetic space, failing at points to earn their grandiose conjecture. In the Ashberyan but unmoored mélange of 'The Aerial Orchids', say, or when 'The Shearer and the Lamb' opens

> 1. [6 v 05]
>
> Above the roof-tree is
> sky in torment where
> birds rage and angels...

it seems difficult to find the 'honest participant in human relationships' which the blurb rightly discovers in Pople's more successful poetry.

These criticisms, though, should not be allowed to eclipse Pople's valuable success in creating a series of delicate worlds in which ways of being can be explored with a genuine insight and innovation:

> Between the motorway
> edge and the dead
> ground lies water –
> between the railway
>
> tracks imprinted
> snow – is to see
> in one way and remember
> in another understand
>
> and store differently –
> an original under
> the lid of a petrol
> station photocopier

(from 'Confessions')

JOEY CONNOLLY

A REAL BOOK

The Ecco Anthology of International Poetry, edited by Ilya Kaminsky and Susan Harris (Ecco Press) £12.99

Published with a view to its use by high school and college students in North America, this anthology has the broader aim of attempting to widen the general audience for poetry in translation. Essentially a chronology of international poetry in the twentieth century, it presents a range of voices from around the globe, from canonical modernists such as Attila Joszef and César Vallejo, to poets of the post-war, post-colonial period (Joseph Brodsky, Ko Un, Anna Kamienska, Léopold Sédar Senghor) and includes the work of younger, more contemporary poets whose work is likely to be less well-known, if known at all, to an English-speaking audience. On the evidence of this book, Anglophone readers and poets would do well to acquaint themselves with an exceptional range of poetry that has been made available in English, in some cases for the first time, by these gifted translations. The wit and virtuosity evident on every page raise the book to the level of a modern anthological classic. Miriam Van Hee, Valzhyna Mort, Guillermo Saavedra, Marcin Swietlicki, Zhang Er and Patrizia Cavalli are just some of the poets who were new to this reader and whose work he has immediately sought out elsewhere. Of course, good anthologies do not exist without a large degree of editorial flair and shrewdness, and Ilya Kaminsky and Susan Harris are to be commended as much for their skill in selection as for their consistency and commitment. In his introduction Kaminsky cites Auden's 'a real book is one that also reads us', and it is worth reiterating too that a good anthology is one that celebrates the encounter between reader and individual text. Its genuine and lasting contribution may derive, to paraphrase Anna Akhmatova, from the brief, sideways glance at a compelling and seductive momentum.

GERRY MCGRATH

WORLDS TO SWING

SIÂN HUGHES, *The Missing* (Salt) £12.99
ELLEN PHETHEAN, *Breath* (Flambard) £7.00
HILARY MENOS, *Berg* (Seren) £7.99

The title of this review – of a trio of first collections – draws on a phrase from a tender, intense poem by Hugh MacDiarmid, with a girl 'Singing till a bairnie / That was nae langer there'. The poem is called 'Empty Vessel'. Siân Hughes' *The Missing* begins with the desire to 'let you into my world'. Its opening stanzas are not empty vessels, but crammed, often whimsically, with objects, overflowing from line to line: 'her memoirs, bath books/ ... and all the stuff in the attic'. Yet a poem crowded with grotesque incident, in which a man in drag fakes pregnancy with 'a striped pillow', can swing suddenly to fellow-passengers, 'too quietly dressed now, shy, undramatised'. Dramatisation – with extraordinary control – allows Hughes' poetry to enfold the crises of her world. Dangerous childbirth is compared to a farm catastrophe: 'the vet / running in – rope in one hand'. The panic surrounding her own child's illness is conveyed through the repeated words of another frantic mother: 'I kept telling them something's wrong'.

Hughes' careful control is at its height in 'The Send-Off', whose pared-down couplets appear to be a dialogue with a living child. 'Sorry we were late. / I brought you a flower. No, it's dead.' But the child is dead, 'The Send-Off' her burial. The poem is, by turns, oblique and directly tender: 'My darling, sleep well in your bed'. It is modern in its understanding of genetic flaws, 'trisomy twenty-one', timeless in its staring-down of death: 'You are a hard lesson to learn'. Hughes' is an unforgettable poetry of grief.

The close of *The Missing* has crumbs of consolation: 'You are not afraid of the storm'. But it also deals, tersely and dramatically, with the end of a relationship, shrunk to electronic messages: 'Delete. Delete'. The collection ends with 'Falling for Elvis', in which his songs instruct the listener 'who not to love'. Both the final sharp tone, and Hughes' reawakened whimsicality, suggest the beginnings of a swing from the deepest world of loss.

The cover notes for Ellen Phethean are a litany of loss: her husband, two close friends. Yet *Breath* begins in childhood, 'the sun setting over Land's End'. The ferocious remembered energy of adults, 'an earthquake that chases / round the house, roaring' is matched by the child: 'an angry boiling sea: a very horrid girl'. Phethean's rhyming can have the swagger of children's songs: 'before I know what I've done / I've cut out my tongue'. It can also be delicate as growth: 'between yes / and no, when desire / breathes on glass'.

Childhood's South is balanced by an adult home, 'the cold North's kiss ... my flinty city'. Phethean's evocations of this troubled city seem to me most powerful when they are myth, when the North-East's party girls enter the world of the Bacchantes:

>Blood
>on their hands, they wake
>to the pale-fingered dawn.

Phethean's final chapter, 'Journey', plunges into the world of her grief. But, like *The Missing*, it does so with the highest degree of discipline, of form and feeling. The young hit-and-run driver who killed her husband is addressed, with extraordinary forgiveness, in a straight-talking sonnet:

>You could be anybody's son.
>You'll not forget what you have done.

Poem after poem compels the reader – or listener – with the ring of its rhymes, the tough clarity of its insight:

>We would follow them to hell,
>they deliver agony so well.

Even in first grief, Phethean is alive to the world turning beyond her, as her narrative swings from the mythic Republic of the Dead to the city's life: 'office girls were slipping out for lunch'. It is a tribute to the emotional and technical strength of Phethean's poetry that the book's final line seems as inevitable as breath: 'Let him go'.

Hilary Menos' *Berg* arrives 'like the map of a world / impossible to resist'. I could not resist the exuberant imaginings of the book's opening. 'Pushing the trolley today I have Ingomar the barbarian', and (in a carefree echo of *The Missing*), 'next week I've got Elvis'. Over the horizon, in the title poem, comes the iceberg's 'thousand mile stare', lit by half-rhyme, a demure madness.

Too many surreal visions could pall, but Menos' restless art swings from unabashed writing about sex to tender poems to her children, and through a whole kaleidoscope of travel. A highly confident writer, she is at her best tackling major themes. Here is Marilyn Monroe:

>Every now and then beauty steps forward ...
>And for one brief moment, time itself steps back.

'This is the sweet season' Menos declares with lyric boldness, not of travel or love, but of the country. Her poems bring as powerful a sense of farm, animal and land as the best work of Ted Hughes. She is unsentimental about the world of her farm, seeing birds with delighted exactness, 'Stonechats chip and bounce', anxiously hearing the surreal violence of her neighbours: 'Nick shooting rats / and Kate screaming Stop'. Her poems can become an animal's voice, in the long vowels of a cow's bellow: 'booming, making a sound / like the Partridge Island foghorn'. More resistibly, she declares herself happy to end in an abattoir's 'companionable chill'. I would not wish to exit the world via certain poultry slaughterhouses.

But Menos' poem 'Pastoral' is indeed 'the map of a world', a miniature masterpiece. It is factual about calving ('the vet ... her arm sunk six joints deep'), exhilarated not by surrealism but by birth's violent energy: 'he bucked at her slap'. The poem's final rhythms feel less made than heard, the turnings of a world: 'while the hills all around spun slower / with us at the hub, by the gate, in this makeshift pen'. Menos herself is sharply conscious of the swings within her life, amongst suited professionals at a college reunion, 'thinking of you in the big shed, easing life into a cold world, overalls torn ... stinking of chain oil'.

Hilary Menos' poems set alight many senses. They finally remind me, as do the bravely shifting worlds of each of these collections, of Shakespeare, whose rhythms swing through the seasons of loss, and of lambing: 'Thou met'st with things dying; I with things newborn'.

ALISON BRACKENBURY

SOME CONTRIBUTORS

PETER BLAND published his first book of poems in 1964 and became closely associated with the Wellington Group, which included James K. Baxter and Louis Johnson. Carcanet publish his *Selected Poems*.

JUDITH CHERNAIK is the author of *The Lyrics of Shelley* and four novels. She is founder and director of London's popular Poems on the Underground.

DON COLES was born in Woodstock, Ontario. After studying in Canada and the UK, he had various European addresses until his middle thirties, after which he taught at York University in Toronto. He has published books of poems in Canada, one in the UK, and one in Germany.

THOMAS DAY lectures in English at the University of Central Lancashire. His recent publications include an essay on Katherine Mansfield, the introduction to a special issue of *Literature and Theology*, and an interview with Michael Symmons Roberts in *PNR* 199.

SIMON ECKETT is a poet, novelist and critic.

RACHEL GALVIN teaches at Princeton University. Her poems and translations appear in *The New Yorker*, *McSweeney's*, and *Colorado Review*, among others. A poetry collection, *Pulleys & Locomotion*, was published in 2009.

JOHN GREENING received a Cholmondeley Award in 2008. Recent books include *Poetry Masterclass*, *Elizabethan Love Poets* and *Hunts: Poems 1979–2009*. His collection *To the War Poets* will appear from OxfordPoets/Carcanet in 2013.

ROBERT GRIFFITHS has published essays in *Acumen* and poetry in *The Rialto*, *Smith's Knoll*, *The Spectator* and other magazines. He lives in Surrey and professionally is a home dad.

HESTER KNIBBE was born in 1946 in Harderwijk, the Netherlands. Her poems have been widely published and have received numerous national awards, including the A. Roland Holst prize in 2009. Her most recent books include *Oogsteen*, a selection of her work from 1982 to 2008, and *Het hebben van schaduw*, both published by De Arbeiderspers, Amsterdam.

JANET KOFI-TSEKPO's poems have been included in *New Poetries V* (Carcanet, 2011), *Ten* (Bloodaxe/Spread the Word, 2010), *Magma*, *Wasafiri* and *Poetry Review*. She works as a writer and facilitator in London.

ADRIAN MAY's books include *Myth and Creative Writing: The Self-Renewing Song* (Longmans, 2010), *KJV – Old Text, New Poetry* (editor, Wivenbooks, 2011), and *Ballads of Bohemian Essex* (poems, Wivenbooks, 2011).

BERNARD O'DONOGHUE is a Fellow of Wadham College, Oxford, where he teaches Medieval Literature. His most recent collection of poems is *Farmers Cross* (Faber, 2011).

JACQUELYN POPE is the author of *Watermark*, published by Marsh Hawk Press (New York). Her poems and translations from Dutch and Afrikaans have appeared in journals in the US and elsewhere.

CHRIS PREDDLE's second collection is *Cattle Console Him* (Waywiser, 2010). He has retired from libraries and lives on a windy shoulder of the Pennines in West Yorkshire.

CAROL RUMENS' most recent collections are *Blind Spots* (2009) and *De Chirico's Threads* (2010), both from Seren. She is a Professor of Creative Writing at Bangor and Hull Universities, and a Fellow of the Royal Society of Literature.

MAURICE RUTHERFORD was born in Hull, and now lives in nearby Bridlington. Following the demise of Peterloo, his New and Selected Poems, *And Saturday is Christmas*, was published in March 2011 by Shoestring Press.

MARK RYAN SMITH lives in Shetland with his wife and two daughters. He works at the county archives and is a part-time doctoral student at the University of Glasgow.

ANNE STEVENSON is an American long resident in Britain, whose *Poems 1955–2005*, published by Bloodaxe in 2006, has won her, among other prizes, a Lanan Life Achievement Award and The Neglected Master's Award from the Poetry Society of America. She has published fourteen collections, the most recent of which is *Stone Milk* (Bloodaxe, 2007).

N.S. THOMPSON's latest book of poetry, the long verse epistle *Letter to Auden* (Smokestack, 2010), has received enthusiastic reviews. His translation of Vivian Lamarque's major poetic sequence *Questa quieta polvere* (*This Quiet Dust*) appears in the current issue of *Journal of Italian Translation* (V, 2).

JANE YEH's first collection, *Marabou*, was shortlisted for the Whitbread, Forward and Jerwood Aldeburgh poetry prizes. Her next book, *The Ninjas*, is due from Carcanet in 2012.

Subscribe to
P·N·Review

I should like to subscribe to *P N Review* for

1 year 6 issues

PERSONAL		INSTITUTIONAL	
£36.00	US $86.00	£43.00	US $105.00

ADD £12 OR US $25 FOR AIRMAIL

2 years 12 issues

PERSONAL		INSTITUTIONAL	
£69.00	US $155.00	£84.00	US $200.00

ADD £24 OR US $50 FOR AIRMAIL

Specimen copy £6.99 / US $14.00

NAME

ADDRESS

POST CODE

I enclose a cheque/po made payable to *PN Review* for

I wish to pay by Visa/MasterCard/Maestro (delete as applicable): SECURITY NO.

NAME ON CARD   EXPIRY DATE

SIGNATURE

to P N Review, Alliance House, 30 Cross Street, Manchester M2 7AQ, UK